D1266669

CHURCH LIBRARY

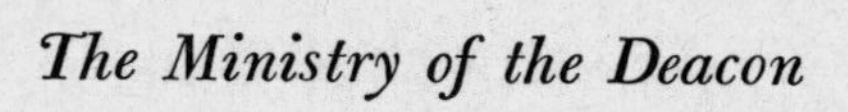

The Ministry of the Deacon

THE MINISTRY OF THE DEACON

By

HOWARD B. FOSHEE

Convention Press

NASHVILLE TENNESSEE

5116-09

Code Number: Church Study Course
This book is Number 1609 in category 16, section
for Adults and Young People

Library of Congress catalog number: 68-13564
Printed in the United States of America
20. o 68 R.R.D.

DEDICATED

TO MY WIFE

ZOLA

About the Author

HOWARD B. FOSHEE was born in Birmingham, Alabama, May 20, 1925. He attended elementary school in Birmingham and graduated from high school in Montgomery, Alabama. Mr. Foshee spent three years in the U. S. Navy during World War II. He received his A. B. degree from Samford University. He holds a B. D. degree from Southern Baptist Theological Seminary, Louisville, Kentucky. Additional study was completed at the School of Journalism, University of Alabama.

Mr. Foshee has served as minister of education for two churches in North Carolina: Asheboro Street Baptist Church, Greensboro; First Baptist Church, Durham.

In April, 1956, he joined the Baptist Sunday School Board as editor of church administration materials. In 1958, he was asked to serve as secretary of the Church Administration Department.

He has been editor of *Church Administration* since the magazine was reactivated in October, 1958. Mr. Foshee has written for various Southern Baptist publications and has served as conference leader across the nation.

He attends Crievewood Baptist Church, Nashville, Tennessee. He has served in various leadership capacities, including the deaconship, at Crievewood.

Contents

Church Study Course

THE CHURCH STUDY COURSE began October 1, 1959. It is a merger of three courses previously promoted by the Sunday School Board: the Sunday School Training Course, the Graded Training Union Study Course, and the Church Music Training Course. On October 1, 1961, the Woman's Missionary Union principles and methods studies were added. On January 1, 1967, the Brotherhood Commission principles and methods studies were added.

The course is fully graded. The system of awards provides a series of five diplomas of twenty books each for Adults or Young People, two diplomas of five books each for Intermediates, and two diplomas of five books each for Juniors.

The course is comprehensive, with books grouped into twenty-one categories. The purpose of the course is to help Christians to grow in knowledge and conviction, to help them to grow toward maturity in Christian character and competence for service, to encourage them to participate worthily as workers in their churches, and to develop leaders for all phases of church life and work.

The Church Study Course is promoted by the Baptist Sunday School Board, 127 Ninth Avenue, North, Nashville, Tennessee 37203, through its Sunday School, Training Union, Church Music, and Church Administration departments; by the Woman's Missionary Union, 600 North Twentieth Street, Birmingham, Alabama 35203; by the Brotherhood Commission, 1548 Poplar Avenue, Memphis, Tennessee 38104; and by the respective departments in the states affiliated with the Southern Baptist Convention. A description of the course and the system of awards may be found in the leaflet "Trained Workmen," which may be obtained without charge from any one of these departments.

A record of all awards earned should be maintained in each church. A person should be designated by the church to keep the files. Forms for such records may be ordered from any Baptist Book Store.

Requirements for Credit for Class or Home Study

IF CREDIT is desired for the study of this book in class or by the home study method, the following requirements must be met:

I. CLASS METHOD

1. The class must meet a minimum of six clock hours. The required time does not include assembly periods.
2. A class member who attends all class sessions and reads the book will not be required to do any written work.
3. A class member who is absent from one or more class sessions must read the book and answer the questions on all chapters he misses.
4. The teacher should request an award for himself. A person who teaches a book in sections for Intermediates or Juniors of any category or conducts an approved unit of instruction for Nursery, Beginner, or Primary children will be granted an award in category 11, Special Studies, which will count as an elective on his own diploma. He should specify in his request the name of the book taught or unit conducted for Nursery, Beginner, or Primary children.

   Credit will be given to "team teachers" when they cooperatively plan the teaching procedures and attend and share responsibility in each teaching session.
5. The teacher should complete the "Request for Book Award" (Form 151) and forward it to the Church Study Course Awards Office, 127 Ninth Avenue, North, Nashville, Tennessee 37203.

II. INDIVIDUAL HOME STUDY

1. A person who does not attend any class session may receive credit by answering all questions for written work as indicated in the book or in a designated periodical. When a person turns in his paper on home study, he must certify that he has read the book.
2. Students may find profit in studying the text together, but individual papers are required. Carbon copies or duplicates in any form cannot be accepted.

3. Home Study work papers may be graded by the pastor or a person designated by him, or they may be sent to the Church Study Course Awards Office for grading. The form entitled "Request for Book Award" (Form 151) must be used in requesting awards. It should be mailed to the Church Study Course Awards Office, 127 Ninth Avenue, North, Nashville, Tennessee 37203.

4. Credit for home study of mission study books not containing questions is earned by writing a synopsis of each chapter.

III. Credit for This Book

This book is number 1609 in category 16, section for Adults and Young People.

Preface

NO ONE PERSON ever writes a book. One individual may write the manuscript, but the concepts are hammered out through years of reading and conversation. A chance remark by a total stranger or a sentence in the morning paper sometimes strikes home and stimulates an idea. Most books evolve rather than burst forth in full regalia.

The Ministry of the Deacon was twelve years in moving from concept to printer's ink. It is a book that developed through intense discussions with many pastors and deacons across the nation. The concepts evolved as thousands of persons have participated in deacon conferences, retreats, and Ridgecrest and Glorieta Baptist Assembly sessions.

The New Testament does not provide specific direction regarding the work that deacons are to perform. Neither does a study of church history answer the question about what a deacon is to do. Deacons have served wherever their churches have assigned special work for them to do.

Today's deacon does many different jobs. In some churches, deacons serve primarily in the administrative areas of finance, properties, and personnel management. And they have served well here. In other churches, the deacons have unfortunately become boards of directors.

In recent years many church leaders have sensed the need for a nucleus of committed persons to lead churches to become dynamic witnessing and ministering fellowships. No other single group seems better qualified than the deacons to lead the crusade for spiritual renewal within the churches.

The purpose of this book is to challenge churches to take a new look at the ministry of the deacon today.

HOWARD B. FOSHEE

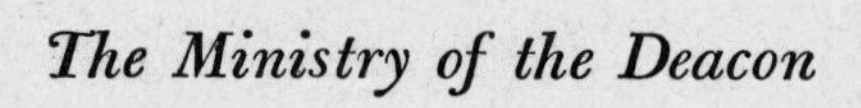
The Ministry of the Deacon

1

Deacons Yesterday and Today

TODAY'S DEACON is a spiritual kinsman to legions of other deacons who have served their generations well. History has marked some deacons for prominence. Many others who have served valiantly are known only to those whose lives have been enriched by their service.

I. DEACONS IN THE NEW TESTAMENT

1. *Understanding the Word "Deacon"*

Paul used words that were familiar to those who heard him. Often, however, he breathed dynamic new meaning into his words. He raised the word *diakonos* (servant) to a lofty spiritual dimension. To understand the change in meaning it is necessary to understand the history of the period in which Paul lived.

Rome, like a giant octopus, encircled most of Europe and the Middle East. Roman military and economic tentacles possessed crushing power. Field commanders wielded disciplined soldiers as an expert chess player handles pawns. Any person or group demonstrating a threat to established governmental power was quickly eliminated.

Local politicians sold their integrity to Rome for a measure of power. Life was cheap. Men spat the word "servant" as they did the word "leper" or "gentile." Often a person's social status was measured by the number of slaves (servants) he owned.

The word "servant" (deacon) was reclaimed from its lowly connotation, and it was enriched with a new and loftier meaning. As a result of this transition, a new concept of spiritual leadership was introduced.

Jesus, for example, taught that the test of greatness for spiritual leaders is not power, authority, or influence. He said "He that is greatest among you shall be your servant. And whosoever shall exalt himself shall be abased; and he that shall humble himself shall be exalted" (Matt. 23:11–12).

The word "deacon" comes from the Greek word *diakonos*. It was taken from the Greek language and made directly into our English word. Thirty times the word *diakonos* is used in the Greek New Testament, but only on five occasions is it translated as "deacon" in the King James Version. When not translated "deacon," *diakonos* is translated minister or servant.

Diakonos literally means "through dust." Although the origin of the word is questioned, the concept of raising dust suggests a servant hastening to serve or to wait on his master.

2. *Choosing the "Seven"*

The seven men appointed in Acts 6 were not called deacons. They were seven mature Christian men asked by the Jerusalem church to help solve a specific emergency. These men provide the first evidence of the apostles' sharing their heavy load with other persons in the church.

It is generally assumed that the "seven" were the prototype of today's deacon. At no place in the New Testament are the seven called deacons.

The churches of the New Testament were not formal institutions owning elaborate buildings. They had neither a complex organizational structure nor large paid staffs. Instead, the churches were dynamic, living groups which reflected the spiritual light of God's love. They were guided by the Holy Spirit, whose power was evident in many ways. Christian fellowship was a paramount characteristic of these early groups.

Cultural and social differences brought about the first threats of disharmony. The church in Jerusalem was composed of persons from various backgrounds.

The two major groups were the Palestinian Jews who adhered to local customs and the other Jews who followed customs of the Greco-Roman culture. Even a difference in language existed between the groups. These barriers tended to build walls of separation.

Acts 6:1 records the eruption which came when the needy widows of Greek (Hellenists) heritage complained that the widows of Palestinian background were receiving a larger portion of the resources made available by the church. This seemingly small complaint was only a symptom of a much larger difficulty. The fellowship of these Christians was being threatened.

The leaders had not faced such a problem before. The breach needed to be healed in a manner that would not impair proclamation of the gospel.

Seven men were selected to solve the specific problem that existed in the Jerusalem church. These men did their job well. The spirit of fellowship within the church was restored, and the proclamation of the gospel continued. The church was blessed. "And the word of God increased; and the number of the disciples multiplied in

Jerusalem greatly; and a great company of the priests were obedient to the faith" (Acts 6:7).

These seven men dealt with a serious problem for which the twelve disciples felt deep concern. But at the time, it seemed best for the disciples to turn to the seven to handle the problem. There are many situations in churches today where deacons by virtue of their temperament or background can serve ably.

The evidence of the prior working of the Holy Spirit in the lives of the seven seems important. This working of the Spirit was evidenced in the seven just as it was in the twelve disciples.

As the word of God increased when the Holy Spirit opened the way for the seven, so we see the beginning of an ever enlarging group of lay leaders learning how to let the Holy Spirit operate through them.

3. *A Service Formalized*

As time passed, the word "deacon" came to have specific meaning.

In the later pastoral epistles, the word "deacon" is used as a noun to designate a more formal service. Philippians 1:1 seems to refer to special leaders or officers of the church: "Paul and Timotheus, the servants of Jesus Christ to all the saints in Christ Jesus which are at Philippi, with the bishops and *deacons.*"

By the end of the second century, as the clergy began to develop into a more structured hierarchy, the deacon was caught up in the movement. He gradually moved from a place of lay servant to a position on the lowest rung of the clerical ladder. Gradually, deacons became a part of the professional clergy.

The deacon by the end of the fourth century had in many places become a formal part of the clergy. Like other members of the clergy, deacons were forbidden to marry. They also wore a distinctive garb which indicated levels of attainment in the clergy.

As needs changed, various duties were assigned deacons. Some were charged with preaching, instructing in the catechism, and distributing food to the needy.

Occasionally today the question is raised regarding deaconesses. Were there deaconesses in the early churches? Are deaconesses needed today?

J. Morris Ashcraft, professor at Midwestern Baptist Theological Seminary, wrote in *Church Administration* (March, 1966):

> Phoebe from the church of Cenchrea was designated a diakonon "of the Church of Cenchrea" in Romans 16:1. On the basis of this, some churches have designated women to the office of "deaconess."
>
> Two translations are possible. Either Phoebe was a "servant" in the general sense or she was a "woman deacon." Those insisting that this is the basis for "deaconesses" point out that the details are quite specific and a deaconess is to receive a special welcome. Some translations such as the Revised Standard Version prefer the translation "deaconess." The term "women" of 1 Timothy 3:11 seems to suggest an order of women parallel to deacons. According to Pliny, there were deaconesses in the churches of Bithynia early in the second century, and deaconesses would have been particularly helpful in dealing with the women members of the churches.
>
> Those who object to the translation "deaconess" point out that the word in Romans 16:1 is masculine in form and a feminine counterpart does not appear in the New Testament, and that the general usage "servant" is preferable here and has considerable parallel usage. Most translators prefer "servant" in Romans 16:1. The women of 1 Timothy 3 are not called deaconesses, and the specific qualifications for deacons in that epistle would eliminate women.

Women are equipped by temperament to serve in a pastoral ministry. In view, however, of the unparalleled service opportunities in the mission action program of Woman's Missionary Union, there seems small need for electing deaconesses today. To do so could only add overlapping organizational structure that might actually lead to a decrease in service. A recent survey indicated that only a small number of Baptist churches have deaconesses today.

II. A Heritage of Stalwart Service

The king of Sparta once said to a royal visitor, "There is the city before you."

The guest quickly remarked, "I am surprised to see that Sparta has no walls."

"Come," replied the king, "I will show you Sparta's walls." With sweeping gesture toward 10,000 soldiers standing tall before them, the Spartan king spoke proudly, "There are the walls of Sparta."

Across the pages of Christian history, an army of loyal deacons has marched. Arm in arm with their pastors, they have served their churches.

William W. Lancaster, Baptist pastor, shared an experience that expresses the bonds of fellowship and service that have bound pastors and deacons together through the years.

"Ministers seem to have a propensity for discouragement. Often they have their own private juniper tree where they, like Elijah of old, can retire to nurse their despair. I had had a particularly rough day. The counseling sessions had been long and tedious. Hospital visits and a death call took precedence over the few minutes that were allotted for meditation and study. To add to that, several negative words had come from individuals who did not like certain changes in the educational program. By the end of the day I had about 'had it.' And in my physical exhaustion I had arrived at another of those points of wondering if my ministry had any thrust.

"It was about that time that Tom, a deacon, came into the office. Tom is one of those rare gems in a church. He is a man's man, a tough customer when it comes to his own personal religious convictions. He has a deep sense of humor and an uncanny ability to look at a man and know what he is thinking. He plopped in an office chair and listened while I blew off steam. When I had finished my complaint session about my long day and my discouragement, he arose with that knowing grin, walked to the door, and looked back at me with a twinkle in his eye. 'I don't know what you are going to do about it, Pastor,' he said, 'but as for me and my house we are going to serve the Lord.'

"With that blunt comment made in love, he walked out the door. He put me in my place, elevated my spirits, and got me out from under the juniper tree. It takes a man of God to do that, and I thank God today for all the deacons in my ministry who have lifted me up and pushed me forward."

Deacons have played a stalwart role in the advancement of Christ's kingdom. Each deacon is a debtor to others who have labored before him.

Deacons, yesterday and today, are part of a noble heritage of service.

Grady C. Cothen, president, Oklahoma Baptist University, tells of a dedicated deacon.

"Years ago, a man came into our church who on the surface appeared to be unimpressive. His educational background was sketchy. He was not a particularly brilliant man nor did he seem to possess many qualifications of leadership. Across the years in our church, he became one of its most influential leaders. This was accomplished by the contagious nature of his Christian dedication and humility. Whatever job the church undertook, he would fit into that part of it which he could do best and lend his influence toward accomplishing the rest. Many times I felt the biblical passage had reference to him which says, 'Be thou faithful unto death, and I will give thee a crown of life' (Rev. 2:10).

"Whatever the issue, you could count on his being on the right side. He was unobtrusive, unassuming, and yet his Christlike spirit thrust him to the forefront in the congregation. It was inevitable that he should become a deacon, in which capacity he served with great distinction over an extended number of years. When he rotated off, after a year he was always reelected. In short, he was a spiritual leader by virtue of his dedication to Christ and his task."

III. Qualifications for the Deacon

Before an athlete is invited to serve on an Olympic team, he must first prove himself as a disciplined competitor. In like manner, Paul believed that a person must have attained spiritual maturity before a church should consider him for deacon service.

A list of personal qualifications for deacons is set forth in the Bible. As every student of a foreign language knows, he first is taught to conjugate the verb "to be."

This knowledge then opens up the new language to him. So it is in developing a Christian life. One must first seek to become what Christ desires him to be. Spiritual maturity comes only by seeking to become more like Christ.

Far more concern is expressed in the Bible about the spiritual qualities that a deacon is to possess than what specific duties he is to perform.

Paul's experience with young churches led him to realize that deacons must be persons of strong spiritual quality. Surrounded by a pagan world, the young churches were tossed about by the evil influences that encompassed them. Paul was unyielding in his concern that deacons possess qualities of Christian character.

An examination of some of the qualifications that the Bible sets forth is illuminating. The biblical requirements are easily divided into positive and negative qualities. Let us first examine some of the positive ones.

1. *Christian Purpose*

Paul wrote to Timothy: "Likewise must the deacons be grave" (1 Tim. 3:8).

Semnos (grave) is derived from a root word meaning to reverence or to worship. Paul sought to indicate that a deacon should possess Christian purpose. Persons coming into a deacon's presence should feel his reverence for spiritual matters.

Our present connotation of the word "grave" does not possess the depth of meaning of the Greek word *semnos* that Paul used. Today's implication of listlessness and gloominess is far from Paul's idea. Because a deacon reveres spiritual matters does not mean that he will be lacking in optimism and humor. Every pastor can relate stories of deacons who enjoyed a good laugh—sometimes on the preacher. James O. Duncan, Baptist editor, illustrates this point by telling this incident.

"I had been pastor of a church for about a year and a half after leaving the seminary and was running out of sermons. I decided I had an answer to my problem of preaching some sermons that I had already preached. I thought I would do the congregation a favor by letting them choose which sermons they wanted to hear. So very boldly I suggested that during one month I would preach again some of the sermons that I had already delivered and for the congregation to simply indicate which ones they wanted to hear. A few days went by and no one responded to my request. Finally, one good deacon with a good sense of humor said that he had heard a sermon that he wanted to hear preached again. I immediately felt that I had really succeeded, but the deacon was having difficulty remembering which sermon it was. Finally, after several minutes of talking back and forth and trying to identify the sermon, the deacon said: 'Oh, I remember which sermon it was now. It was one I heard while I was on vacation in Florida.' I had learned a good lesson, and the deacon and I had shared in a good laugh."

2. *Spiritual Integrity*

"Holding the mystery of the faith in a pure conscience" (1 Tim. 3:9). Sound doctrinal conviction should characterize a deacon. His spiritual integrity is beyond reproach. He is firm in his convictions. Never can it be said of a deacon that he is "tossed to and fro, and carried about with every wind of doctrine." (Eph. 4:14).

Paul exhorted the elders: "Take heed to yourselves and to all the flock, in which the Holy Spirit has made you guardians, to feed the church of the Lord which he obtained with his own blood" (Acts 20:28, RSV).

3. *Proved Spiritual Maturity*

"Let these also first be proved; then let them use the office of a deacon, being found blameless" (1 Tim. 3:10). Paul advised that a man should demonstrate his spiritual qualifications before being elected to serve as a deacon. His daily conduct and speech should be observed for an appropriate period by fellow Christians. Only if he has proved his spiritual maturity should he be elected.

"Proved" carries with it the idea of testing. As products and materials are pretested, so should a deacon prove himself as one who is spiritually worthy. His life is beyond accusation. He has been tested and found true.

4. *Christian Family Life*

"Let the deacons be husbands of one wife, ruling their children and their own houses well" (1 Tim. 3:12). This verse is probably one of the most controversial statements regarding deacon qualifications. Because of its nature, a more detailed interpretation is in order. William E. Hull has written in *Church Administration* (December, 1961):

Despite endless argument over the meaning of this simple statement (1 Tim. 3:12), it is clear that it insists on at least three things.

First, it demands that a deacon maintain a healthy view of the home. In the early church there were those who forbade marriage as an evil in the sight of God (1 Tim. 4:3). . . . The deacon is to reject such false asceticism by embracing the biblical emphasis on marriage as a calling within the will of God.

Second, this passage enjoins a complete break with pagan standards of marriage. Bigamy or polygamy is obviously condemned. Beyond this, any type of immoral, extramarital relationship, so prevalent in the Greco-Roman world of the first century, is repudiated. The deacon is to be a model of faithful devotion to one wife.

Third, this verse reminds the deacon of his commitment to the sanctity of the marriage bond. Behind this passage lies the teaching of Jesus with its absolute rejection of divorce (Mark 10:2–12). Not only must the divorce court be unknown to a deacon, but anything which threatens to corrupt or to destroy the perfect unity of marriage must be resisted and defeated.

The Bible also stresses high qualifications for the deacon's wife: "Even so must their wives be grave, not slanderers, sober, faithful in all things" (1 Tim. 3:11). Some able scholars interpret the grammatical construction of this sentence to be a reference to any woman who is to be considered for a similar position of Christian leadership.

The Bible also stresses some qualifications from a negative stance.

5. *Honest in Speech*

"Not double-tongued" (1 Tim. 3:8). Paul used a word *dilogos* which is translated two tongued or double-tongued. *Di* means two or double. *Logos* means word or speaking. As these two words are put together, we get Paul's connotation of two words or double-tongued.

A deacon should be in control of his tongue. He should speak out for righteous causes. He also has a responsibility for being slow to anger. His word is always honest. Gossip, talebearing, idle talking, and slander are not a part of his nature.

6. *Temperate in Living*

"Not given to much wine" (1 Tim. 3:8). Christians of the first century lived in a world of pagan excesses. Paul spoke forth boldly that Christians must be stewards of good influence. "Whatsoever ye do, do all to the glory of God" (1 Cor. 10:31).

Every deacon will be under surveillance by non-Christians. His life should be free from any excesses that would injure him and his family, and make ineffective his witness. Deacons today should abstain from the use and sale of alcoholic beverages.

7. *Steward of Possessions.*

"Not greedy of filthy lucre" (1 Tim. 3:8). Material possessions are not necessarily evil or filthy. Paul did not have this in mind when he set forth this qualification. Instead, he focused attention on a person's attitude toward material possessions. Rather than being one who has an obsession for material possessions, a deacon should be motivated to do the will of God. When a person seeks to do God's will, his heart will be filled with compassion; and he will desire to share his possessions with others.

IV. Church Guidelines for Effective Deacon Service

There are basic guidelines that a church should remember as it considers the work of deacons.

1. *Maintain Biblical Qualifications*

Churches should always adhere to the scriptural qualifications for deacons. It is easy for local tradition to establish man-made qualifications rather than to uphold God-given spiritual qualities.

Churches will always be tempted to lower their standards for deacons. Paul indicated that a person should already have attained the required spiritual qualifications prior to election. He said: "Let these also first be proved." Before a man is considered for election, he should already have attained spiritual maturity.

Every Christian should, of course, continue to grow in Christ. Like Paul, the deacon will have concern "for the equipment of the saints, for the work of ministry, for building up the body of Christ, until we all attain to the unity of the faith and of the knowledge of the Son of God, to mature manhood, to the measure of the stature of the fulness of Christ" (Eph. 4:12–13, RSV).

2. *Choose Men Who Can Serve Well*

In addition to seeking spiritually qualified persons, a church should also recognize that some persons are more adept at serving in the area of pastoral ministries than others. As persons are being considered as possible deacon candidates, the work that will be required of them should also be kept in focus. Choose qualified men who have or who can develop skills in witnessing, counseling, visiting, ministering, maintaining fellowship, and interpreting the work of the church to others.

Some individuals are more at ease serving in areas of finance, properties management, or personnel administration. But if deacons are to perform the task of serving with the pastor in performing the church's pastoral ministries, they need to be individuals who have a disposition for this type of service. Many men have talents which can enable them to serve their church competently.

A. Donald Bell, professor, Southwestern Baptist Theological Seminary, once told of a flash flood in a community where he was serving as interim pastor. The church building became a relief center for meeting the needs in this crisis. Bell said: "One outstanding deacon in the church, a man who was meticulous in dress and personal appearance, had labored tirelessly in the flood areas, helping people and trying to protect the properties. I had decided to attempt to hold prayer meeting at the scheduled time although we had no idea of the response. The fact of the matter is, I had been working in the flood area that same day.

"As time for prayer meeting rolled around, a few of the faithful ones who were able to attend gathered at the church. Just as I was ready to open the service, this faithful deacon walked into the room. The response of the people was both humorous and serious. For here this distinguished gentleman, chairman of deacons and always so precise in his dress and grooming, stood like a laboring hand direct from the fields. His clothes were drenched with flood waters and his boots were covered with mud. He hung his head and walked in apologetically. Before he took his seat, he was so conscious of his appearance that he attempted to apologize publicly to the people there.

"I interrupted with these words, 'My dear brother deacon, I do not believe that in the history of our church any deacon has ever been better dressed for the ministries of his service than you are dressed right now in this prayer meeting!' "

3. *Choose Men Who Can Work Well with Others*

A person who cannot work with others will probably not serve ably as a deacon. Much of the work of today's deacons calls for a double portion of patience and understanding.

A deacon needs a sensitive spirit if he is to experience a deep compassion and empathy for those whom he serves. But he must not have an overly sensitive skin, that is, he cannot get his feelings hurt easily.

Christian maturity should be one of his chief characteristics. He needs the ability to disagree in an agreeable tone and manner.

When a final decision is made by fellow deacons or the congregation, he will give his full support even though he may have voted against the recommendation.

4. *Choose Men Who Will Train for Service*

A journal gave this advice for its employees who were engaged in a rapidly emerging business of space engineering. The employees were urged to "train, retrain, reeducate, or die." The advice was sound. Rapid obsolescence today requires constant learning and relearning in order to cope with new frontiers of knowledge.

Since the work of the deacon has changed rapidly in recent years from church business administration to pastoral ministries, new skills must be learned. Old patterns of thought and work habits need rethinking in order to serve Christ in a new dimension.

Before a person is elected a deacon, a church should consider whether he will engage in special training opportunities for deacons. There is unique deacon work to be done that requires specific training. A deacon should participate in the organization of his church, but the heavy weight of his deacon work will not permit him to carry excessive leadership positions. To be elected a deacon is more than an honor. It is a charge to assume a major assignment of high priority.

Training for deacon service is being stressed by churches more fervently than ever before. Churches should consider only those individuals who will seek to become skilled servants of Christ and their church.

Deacons should participate in training sessions in order to develop into skilled and dedicated servants of their church.

(1) *Benefits of deacon training.*—Many benefits accrue from training deacons to understand, appreciate, and perform their jobs. Training helps to:

a. Strengthen the foundation for deacon service.—Training deacons to perform their responsibilities in pastoral ministries can bridge the chasms that develop as deacons move from work in properties, finances, and church staff administration. Training can prepare a solid foundation for deacons to understand better their specific job and related jobs. Without a solid foundation of understanding and appreciation for their new work, conflicts will arise.

b. Heighten deacon morale.—Human emotions are such that morale fluctuates like a thermometer in early spring. Training can increase morale as deacons attain a sense of achievement in a job well done.

c. Decrease deacon dropouts.—Dropouts from active deacon service occur most often when people do not appreciate and understand their work. Training can equip a deacon both to enjoy his work and to perform it well.

(2) *Getting ready for deacon training.*—Comprehensive plans should be developed well in advance. Here are some suggestions for starting a deacon training program.

a. Decide on priority training needs.—Take a comprehensive look at all needs. Involve the deacons in a study and discussion of their training needs. Encourage deacons to participate. Isolate long-range needs and determine immediate training priorities.

b. Set goals for training.—Determine what you want to achieve through training. State training goals in such a way that progress can be measured on completion. Be specific regarding the expected outcome of deacon training.

c. Enlist persons to lead training sessions.—Leaders should know their subject and have a knowledge of available resources. Seek leaders who understand adults, the work of the deacon, and the total program of the church. Leaders need to have the ability to get their message across with sincerity and competence.

d. Decide on resource materials.—Examine all proposed training to obtain the finest resource materials. Consider using these resource materials: (1) filmstrip *The Ministry of the Deacon Today,* (2) pamphlet "Deacons in Training," and (3) relevant articles in *Church Administration* concerning the work of deacons.

e. Establish the training schedule.—Place the schedule into the church calendar. Relate all training to the Training Union director since he leads the training program of the church. Consider special training at such times as regular deacons' meeting, special sessions during the week, or deacon retreats on Friday and Saturday.

f. Evaluate the training program.—Evaluate the results objectively with those persons who planned the training. Review the goals and determine if these goals were achieved. Build the results of this evaluation into the next phase of deacon training.

AGENDAS FOR THE TRAINING OF DEACONS

A variety of deacon training agendas can be designed to fit specific time schedules. These sample agendas illustrate the type of sessions that can be planned.

Agenda for Training Session
(*Two and One-half Hours*)

Scripture reading and prayer	*5 minutes*
Introduction of speakers on program (Suggested leader chairman of deacons)	*5 minutes*
"The Pastoral Ministry of Deacons: An Overview" (Suggested leader: pastor)	*30 minutes*
"How to Witness" (Suggested leader: pastor or a church staff member)	*30 minutes*
"The Deacon Assisting in Worship" (Suggested leader: pastor)	*30 minutes*
"How to Minister to the Sick and Bereaved" (Suggested leader: hospital chaplain or a physician)	*30 minutes*
Discussion of "Ministering to the Sick and Bereaved" (Suggested discussion leaders: chaplain, physician, and pastor)	*20 minutes*

Agenda for a Deacons' Retreat

Friday evening	
Scripture reading and prayer	*5 minutes*
"What We Hope to Achieve Through the Retreat"	*5 minutes*
(Suggested leader: chairman of deacons)	
Introduction of speakers on program	*5 minutes*
(Suggested leader: chairman of deacons)	
"The Pastoral Ministry of Deacons: An Overview"	*40 minutes*
(Suggested leader: pastor)	
Discussion groups on "How Can We Strengthen the Pastoral Ministries of Our Church?"	*40 minutes*
Reports from discussion groups	*20 minutes*
(Suggested coordinator: chairman of deacons)	
Saturday morning	
Scripture reading and prayer	*5 minutes*
"How to Witness"	*30 minutes*
(Suggested leader: pastor or a church staff member)	
"How Deacons Can Minister to the Sick"	*40 minutes*
(Suggested leader: physician)	
Relaxation	*20 minutes*
Panel: "Ministering to the Sick and Bereaved"	*30 minutes*
(Suggested panel members: physician, chaplain, and pastor)	
"The Deacon Assisting in Worship"	*30 minutes*
(Suggested leader: pastor)	

2

Evolving Concepts of Deacon Service

THE SCRIPTURES do not list specific duties that deacons are to perform. The Bible focuses on deacon qualifications rather than the exact nature of the work.

Since firm biblical guidelines for service are not established, differing concepts regarding the deacons' work have arisen.

Some of these concepts have gained considerable support. As needs have changed, however, the work of deacons has changed to meet these needs.

I. CONCEPTS REGARDING WORK OF DEACONS

1. *Deacons As Board of Directors*

Sometimes the term "board of deacons" has been used to refer to deacons. How did this term originate?

In the late 1800's, during the rise of the democratic revolution, individual rights began to be considered more seriously. Business problems began to be discussed by groups of persons in an effort to find acceptable solutions. Often these groups met for a meal around a wooden or board table to discuss their problems. By easy transfer of meaning, "board" became identified with any group of persons charged with decision-making. Phrases such as "board of directors" and "board of trustees" soon became a part of daily conversation.

As deacons assumed much of the management of church properties and finances in the late 1800's, the business world concept of "board of directors" was, unfortunately, transferred to the church.

What are evidences in some churches that deacons are operating under the concept of a "board"?

(1) When all major recommendations from church organizations and church committees are screened by the deacons to determine whether they should go to the congregation.

(2) When the pastor and staff members are directly responsible to the deacons rather than to the church.

(3) When the use or expenditure of major church resources, such as facilities and finances, must first be approved by the deacons.

There are no levels of authority in a Baptist church. The congregation, under the leadership of the Holy Spirit, makes the final decision in all matters it considers. The actual authority of deacons is one of Christian influence rather than authority as a board of directors.

Baptist churches make a mistake when they adopt the term "board of deacons." There is no scriptural basis for this concept, and it is in direct conflict with the pattern of congregational government that Baptist churches follow.

2. *Deacons As Business Managers*

Some persons hold a related view that deacons are church business managers. Some harboring this view quote Acts 6:3 as their biblical authority "Look ye out among you seven men . . . whom we may appoint over *this business.*" The Revised Standard Version translates this passage "to this duty." Regardless of the translation, it is important to understand that the passage says "whom we may appoint over *this* business" rather than *the* business. The word "this" refers to the immediate need that was facing the Jerusalem church at that particular time.

How did the concept of deacons as business managers emerge?

During the Reformation, John Calvin began to speak of the deacon as a layman rather than as a member of the clergy. He taught that deacons should assume responsibility for serving others. He instructed deacons to preach and minister to the sick and poor. This pattern of service was followed by many evangelical groups for a long time.

In 1774, the historic Charleston Confession of Faith initiated a change in the theory of the work of deacons. The confession stated that deacons were to be in charge of the "inferior" services of a church. Deacons were admonished to serve at the Lord's table, to collect and dispense for the poor, to aid in maintaining the fellowship of the flock, and to give close attention to relieving the pastor of secular church concerns. This last provision (participation in secular church concerns) was to influence greatly the work of deacons in succeeding years.

R. B. C. Howell, honored Baptist pastor, wrote *The Deaconship* in 1846. This book had wide influence among Baptists, and it heavily influenced the type of work assigned to deacons. Howell's chief premise was that deacons should focus their attention on administering the temporal affairs of the church. He spoke of the deacon working in his separate department—the secular business of the church—while the pastor tended to the spiritual affairs. This concept was widely acclaimed, and many churches assigned all church business responsibilities to deacons.

When Howell's book was published in 1846, most Baptist churches were small and located in rural areas. Many churches did not have a full-time pastor. Worship services were held only once or twice a month. Trained volunteer leaders were few. Without a regular pastor, someone had to manage the building and grounds, finances, and other business details. Since the deacons were often the only elected church officers, they gradually assumed their responsibility.

In the 1920's, Prince E. Burroughs wrote *Honoring the Deaconship*. This book, now out of print, followed the same philosophy set forth by Howell. Written in the form of a study course book, it was studied widely in churches.

Although many churches now have multiple staffs and complex organizational structures, they still assign church business responsibilities to deacons. What are some indications that deacons are operating as church business managers?

(1) When the deacons' responsibilities are composed solely of business management matters.

(2) When deacons administer the affairs of the church primarily as a business operation.

(3) When deacons are viewed as the decision-makers in all business affairs.

(4) When business efficiency becomes more important than Christian growth and service.

3. *Deacons Serving in Pastoral Ministries*

A more acceptable concept of deacon service is emerging. A growing number of churches are asking their deacons to serve alongside the pastor in the pastoral ministries of the church.

Gaines S. Dobbins, distinguished professor, Southern Baptist Theological Seminary and Golden Gate Baptist Theological Seminary, has probably done more than anyone else to call attention to the spiritual ministry of the deacon. In 1929, he wrote *Baptist Churches in Action* (out of print). He called attention to the spiritual qualities the deacon should possess. He referred to the deacon as a "specially qualified man of God called by his church to high and holy scriptural office."

Churches began to restudy the work of deacons. A new spiritual dimension began to evolve. This spiritual role has continued to grow.

As churches have sought to minister more effectively to varying needs of persons, pastors have faced increasing difficulty in meeting the spiritual needs of these individuals in the church and community.

Pastors, seeking to shoulder the full pastoral responsibilities of a church, find the load overwhelming. In other areas of the church's work, church program organizations and committees have assumed much of the work load. But the pastoral work of the church, with its emphasis on the spiritual welfare of the flock, presses in heavily. Many pastors report that their greatest personal need is for colaborers to share in the pastoral ministries. The need is great for qualified and highly motivated persons to share this spiritual ministry with the pastor.

Wayne Dehoney writing about the work of the "seven" in the Jerusalem church said in the November, 1959 issue of *Church Administration:* "The first responsibility of these men was to assist the pastors in the spiritual ministry of shepherding and caring for the flock and to free the pastors for the ministry of prayer, preaching, and training. Actually, these seven were selected to be 'undershepherds' of the flock."

The spiritual qualifications for deacons stress the importance of ministering to the needs of persons. Serving in this capacity enriches the lives of persons, motivates the deacon to greater service, and enables the pastor to give more specific attention to persons in greatest need.

Are deacons needed today? Definitely yes, if a church has distinctive work that can best be done by deacons.

An editorial by J. Terry Young in the state paper *The California Southern Baptist* (April 16, 1964) provides sound guidance concerning the needs that deacons can meet today. He wrote: "Deacons are needed when a church recognizes its responsibilities for a group of persons with physical and spiritual needs to whom the pastor, with normal assistance by laymen, cannot minister adequately. . . . If a church today recognizes within its fellowship a group of people who need a spiritual ministry which cannot be met because of the already heavy responsibility of the pastor, then it should give consideration to ordaining deacons to assist the pastor in this personal ministry."

What are some evidences that deacons are serving in the pastoral work of a church?

(1) When deacons seek to build and maintain Christian harmony and fellowship.

(2) When deacons seek to proclaim the gospel to believers and unbelievers.

(3) When deacons seek to meet the needs of persons in the church and the community.

(4) When deacons care for individuals and families.

(5) When deacons report in their meetings on the sick, the elderly, and others in need.

II. Today's Deacons and Church Tasks

The deacon is a colaborer with his pastor in implementing the church's function of ministry. He does not replace the pastor in performing work that the pastor alone should do. Nor is he merely an assistant to carry out meaningless assignments. Instead, pastor and deacons stand together as partners in a spiritual task. Together they serve in the pastoral ministries of a church.

The doctrine of the priesthood of believers teaches not only that one has access to God without the necessity of going through a human intermediary but also that each believer should perform "priestly" functions of care for fellow Christians. This concern for the spiritual welfare of the flock should be felt by every church member but in an even greater degree by deacons.

If a deacon is to understand his job and its relationships, he needs to understand the tasks of the church he serves.

1. *Definition of Church Tasks*

Church tasks are those basic continuing jobs that a church must perform if it is to be and do what God expects. The achievement of church tasks moves a church toward its objectives. Church tasks are those God-given assignments that must be performed if a church is to be the body of Christ on earth.

There are many activities in which a church engages. But every activity may not be basic to the continuing life of the church. A church task is an action that must be performed if a church is to achieve its full purpose.

Here are some examples of church tasks—those jobs that every church must continue to do.

(1) Proclaim the gospel to believers and unbelievers

(2) Teach the biblical revelation

(3) Train church members to perform the functions of the church

(4) Reach persons for Christ and church membership

(5) Teach missions

(6) Teach music

These statements of church tasks represent some of the basic continuing jobs a church must perform if it is to achieve what Christ intended when he established the church.

Some church tasks are of similar nature. These similar tasks may be grouped. When tasks are grouped, they constitute a program or a service of a church.

2. *Definition of Church Programs and Services*

Church tasks are generally grouped into one of three patterns:

(1) *Church programs.*—A program is comprised of tasks which are of *primary* importance in moving a church toward its objectives. Examples of church programs are: pastoral ministries, Bible teaching program, missions program, training program, and music program.

It is important to note that the deacon's work is a part of the pastoral ministries of a church.

(2) *Church program services.*—A church program service is comprised of those basic, continuing activities

which churches perform to support the carrying out of the program tasks.

The church program services are church library and church recreation.

(3) *Church administrative services.*—A church administrative service is composed of those basic continuing actions of administration which serve the congregation and its leaders.

Administrative services provide church organization, human resources, physical resources, financial resources, and administrative controls. The work is usually implemented through the church council and church officers and committees, such as church clerk, treasurer, trustees, nominating committee, properties committee, personnel committee, stewardship committee, missions committee, public relations committee.

3. *Definition of Pastoral Ministries*

Deacons have responsibility for serving their church in its pastoral ministries.

The four basic tasks of the church's pastoral ministries are:

(1) Proclaim the gospel to believers and unbelievers.

(2) Care for the church's members and other persons in the community.

(3) Lead the church to engage in a fellowship of worship, witness, education, ministry, and application.

(4) Lead the church in performing its tasks

The deacon serves with his pastor in performing these tasks. The pastoral ministries of a church have deep spiritual overtones, and those who execute the tasks must possess unique skill and Christian maturity. The term "pastoral" reflects the biblical symbolism of a loving shepherd watching over his flock. A deacon shares in the intimate spiritual experiences as well as in crises in the lives of persons. In all these experiences, the deacon represents Christ.

Serving with the pastor in meeting the spiritual needs of persons is not an easy assignment. Long hours are often required. Late in the night a telephone may ring at a deacon's home. Time may be spent seeking to help an alcoholic master his problems. Acts of benevolence become a regular part of a deacon's day. He listens to a concerned father and mother as they seek guidance regarding a wayward son. A deacon's worn Bible speaks silently of personal study and Christian witness. He enjoys the warm fellowship with his pastor as they discuss how the ordinances of baptism and the Lord's Supper can become more meaningful to the congregation.

Deacons who measure up to the biblical qualifications are equipped to minister to the spiritual needs of persons. Pastors greatly need and desire the assistance of qualified and highly motivated deacons to serve with them. Together they serve as spiritual allies. They become colaborers in meeting the needs of persons in Jesus' name.

III. Interpretation of Deacons' Work

Pastoral ministries can be broken into a more precise list of subpoints. An enlarged statement of the tasks reveals wide areas of service for the deacons.

The list includes:

(1) Proclaim the gospel to believers and unbelievers

- Participate in the witnessing activities
- Participate in the preaching program

(2) Care for the church's members and other persons in the community
- Minister in times of crises
- Provide pastoral counsel and referral
- Provide vocational guidance
- Perform acts of benevolence

(3) Lead the church to engage in a fellowship of worship, witness, education, ministry, and application.
- Maintain church fellowship
- Lead corporate worship
- Administer ordinances
- Be informed about the life and work of the church
- Set a personal example of Christian living

(4) Lead the church in performing its tasks.
- Interpret the work of the church to church members and the community
- Encourage cooperative work with other churches.

Chapters 3, and 4, and 5 interpret more fully these areas of service.

1. *Relation of Deacons to Pastor and Staff*

The pastor, church staff, and deacons share a common task. They are all partners in performing the pastoral work assigned by their church. As befitting any partners, a spirit of mutual respect, oneness of purpose, and warm bonds of Christian fellowship should exist.

The pastor and staff are responsible to the church.

Each was called by the church and given direction concerning his areas of work. The pastor and staff take direction from the church and report to the church.

The deacons, likewise, are responsible to the church. They report to the congregation on their assigned work and are given direction by the congregation. The pastor or the staff does not supervise the deacons. Neither do the deacons supervise the pastor and the staff.

Every effort should be made to develop and maintain regular and accurate communication. An understanding and appreciation of work assignments is essential. Plans should be developed that are mutually harmonious with, and supportive of, the church's goals and objectives.

The pastor, the staff, and the deacons should pledge to pray for one another as they labor together in Christ. A common responsibility and parentage should strengthen the ties that bind them into a spiritually dynamic and highly motivated team.

2. *Relation of Deacons to Administrative Services*

The Bible is silent regarding the specific work that deacons are to do. In some churches, deacons have had major responsibility for implementing church administrative services. They have performed well in areas of committee work such as finance, properties, personnel, trustees, and insurance. In recent years the concept of deacon service has changed from administrative services work to service of a witnessing and shepherding nature. No one type of work is more spiritual than another. All work done for Christ and his church can be spiritual.

Each church should determine how it desires to get its work done. An ever increasing number of churches are assigning responsibility for administrative services to church committees. Deacons are being asked to serve beside the pastor in pastoral ministries. Churches have discovered, nevertheless, that it is difficult for deacons to carry out both administrative services and pastoral ministries.

In addition to freeing deacons for new areas of service, there are other advantages for establishing church committees to handle administrative service work. Some of the advantages are that committees provide opportunity for: (1) using more persons, thereby establishing a broader base of leadership; (2) persons of special administrative skill to serve their church; (3) women and young adults to serve.

Church committees receive direction from the church and report to the congregation on their work. They do not bring their reports to the deacons for approval before reporting to the congregation. When requested, a church committee should periodically inform the deacons on matters such as finances, properties, and personnel if the information will assist the deacons in performing their work better. Deacons need to understand the work of their church if they are to enlighten others. Regular attendance at business meetings and participation in the life of the church can usually provide much of this needed information.

In small churches, it may be necessary for deacons to administer some of the business affairs. A plan needs to be developed for the establishment of church committees as soon as the church has sufficient leaders to free the deacons to assume their primary responsibility in pastoral ministries.

3. *Relation of Deacons to Church Council*

The church council is the servant of the congregation. It exists, not to make decisions for the congregation, but to help the congregation make its decisions wisely. The church council provides the congregation with a group of responsible leaders to whom it can look for planning, coordinating, and evaluating a church's work.

The responsibilities of the church council differ from the responsibilities of the deacons. The church council's work is to:

(1) Formulate and recommend to the congregation suggested church objectives and goals.

(2) Develop and recommend to the congregation action plans for reaching church goals.

(3) Review and coordinate suggested program plans and actions by church officers, organizations, and committees; and provide for adequate communication among church officers, organizations, and committees.

(4) Review and report as appropriate to the congregation the use of resources in terms of the needs of church programs as they work toward the achievement of the objectives and goals of a church.

(5) Evaluate program achievements in terms of church objectives and goals and report evaluations to the congregation.

Deacons are related to the church council through their chairman. The chairman of deacons serves either as a member of the council or an ex officio member. The author of the pamphlet "The Church Council" (Church Administration Department, Baptist Sunday School Board) says:

Good lines of communication need to be established between the deacons and the church council. They serve the same church members. Each group is responsible to the church and has distinctive services to render. They should share information with each other freely. The deacon chairman, either as a member or as an ex officio member, should take the initiative to meet with the church council to discuss matters of mutual interest regarding their work. The pastor, as chairman of the church council, should see that the deacon chairman has the information he needs about the program plans. The deacon chairman should inform the deacons about the plans of the church programs. This information would enable the deacons to perform their own services more knowledgeably, and would enable both deacons and the church council to relate their work to each other more effectively.

3

Proclaim the Gospel to Believers and Unbelievers

THE QUALITIES required of deacons give credence to a service of significant spiritual dimension. Both the Scriptures and Christian history provide stirring accounts of deacons who were active in witnessing and preaching.

Prior to launching out in service beyond the walls of his church building, each deacon needs a renewing encounter with Christ. Spiritual fires can burn with intensity only after such an experience. The personal devotional life of a deacon must be such that he will lose all desire to be a spectator. He must be drawn into the battle. This chapter interprets the pastoral task of the church "proclaim the gospel to believers and unbelievers."

I. Participating in Witnessing Activities

After the "seven" were chosen by the church in Jerusalem to assist in healing the breach in fellowship, the Scriptures declare that "the word of God increased; and the number of the disciples multiplied in Jerusalem greatly; and a great company of the priests were obedient to the faith" (Acts 6:7).

In addition to remolding the shattered fellowship, these Christian men played a major role in increasing the number of believers.

1. *Deacons Active As Witnesses*

Leonard E. Sanderson, Baptist pastor and evangelist, says: "Some of the outstanding soul-winners of the New Testament are Philip and Stephen, whose names are among these first seven. This should not surprise us because the men selected were 'men of honest report, full of the Holy Ghost and wisdom.' That kind of man of necessity would be a soul-winner. One cannot be full of the Holy Ghost without being concerned for the salvation of the lost. The New Testament norm for deacons is for their ministry to be spiritually centered. This means soul-winning will be the preeminent responsibility, and the conservation of saved souls the next most important task."

Deacons represent one of the greatest untapped spiritual resources in Baptist churches today. There is no measure to fathom the depth of influence deacons can have if each deacon mobilized his Christian witness and used his capacities for Christian witness.

Witnessing is central in the ministry of the deacon. Thousands of deacons would respond like a mighty army if witnessing were stressed as one of their major responsibilities. Just imagine the results if deacons, like Jesus, would say: "To this end have I been born, and to this end am I come into the world, that I should bear witness unto the truth" (John 18:37, ASV).

Deacons were chosen for such a high calling. They have a spiritual kinship with the one who said: "'You did not choose me, but I chose you and appointed you that you should go and bear fruit and that your fruit should abide'" (John 15:16, RSV).

The impact of pastor and deacon witnessing side by side could turn the world upside down. Duke K. McCall, president of Southern Baptist Theological Seminary, once said: "The great evolution in Christendom today is the rediscovery of the layman instead of the clergyman as the cutting edge in Christian witnessing. The preacher's place is to train and inspire the layman to be the cutting edge in witnessing and the saving salt in society. And he has dulled himself as he has tried to be the cutting edge himself. The problem with our churches is we have religion in moderation when what the world needs is some quiet fanatics."

The world waits on deacon-shepherds working in the night searching out lost sheep. But this is not an easy assignment. It requires discipline, compassion, and training. Deacons must understand and accept the fact that Christian witnesses are not always popular. Christ advised: "If the world hate you, ye know that it hateth me before it hateth you. If ye were of the world, the world would love its own" (John 15:18–19). Later he said: "Yea, the time cometh, that whosoever killeth you will think that he doeth God service" (John 16:2).

Witnessing is not new for deacons. Through the centuries some persons have accepted Christ because deacons witnessed to them. Deacons have served well as colaborers with their pastors as together they have witnessed for Christ.

Theodore F. Adams, Baptist pastor, relates: "Some years ago I asked our deacons to join with some others in a program of personal visitation for those who were unsaved or not members of our church. One deacon objected and felt he just could not do it. However, when the deacons approved the plan, he went along since he agreed to cooperate out of pure loyalty to his pastor and the church he loved.

"When the night for the first visiting came, we gathered at the church for supper, for some instructions, and for prayer. Then he went out with another man to visit. They took some visitation cards with them. I'll never forget his return. He walked into the church, waving his cards with a smile on his face and a light in his eyes. He came up to me and said: 'Pastor, that was fun. Let's do it again.' He had had a great time, he had won some folks to Christ—and above all else—he had been given a new understanding of what deacons could do and what they should do in personal visitation in the life of the church."

M. Ray McKay, Baptist pastor and seminary professor, tells a similar incident when he was a pastor. "I began to cultivate this deacon by calling him to accompany me on soul-winning visits in the evening. He was a hard working insurance agent, tired by nightfall. However, he always accepted my invitation, soon became enthusiastic, persistent, and effective. Then he went with another layman, and I took a new man. I have heard him say publicly: 'I was so tired in the evenings when the pastor called I wished he would leave me alone. But when we returned about ten o'clock, I was thoroughly refreshed by the blessings of the Lord. Nothing will restore your energies so quickly as seeing someone trust the Lord as Saviour. When the pastor first came, I could not quote John 3:16. But when we began to try to win lost men, I saw it was important to be able to use the Bible.'"

2. *Deacons Skilled As Witnesses*

An important responsibility of deacons is to win persons to Christ and to lead others to do so. Both training and personal example are important.

Specific training should be provided for all deacons in order to equip them to be more effective witnesses. Emphasis can be given to deacon training at the regular deacons' meeting or at a special retreat or training conference.

Some guidelines to follow may be useful in witnessing.

(1) *Learn some basic Scripture passages.*—Memorize a few of the most basic soul-winning Scripture verses. Learn the location of these verses in your Bible. Your visit will probably be more effective if you read the Scriptures to a person. But learn the verses so that you will be better prepared.

The following are some relevant Scripture verses:

"All have sinned" (Rom. 3:23).

"The wages of sin is death" (Rom. 6:23).

"By grace are ye saved through faith . . . not of works" (Eph. 2:8–9).

"Except ye repent, ye shall all likewise perish" (Luke 13:3).

"Now is the accepted time" (2 Cor. 6:2).

(2) *Relate to the person what Christ has meant to you.*—A simple account of what Christ has done in your life will have much more influence than a formal presentation of ideas that someone else has prepared.

(3) *Cultivate the friendship of the person to whom you are witnessing.*—Get to know him, his background, and his personal interests. Seek to cultivate his fellow-

ship so that he knows that you honestly care about his spiritual condition.

(4) *Depend on God for guidance.*—Private prayer before you make a visit can strengthen you and prepare the heart of the one to whom you will be witnessing. Seek God's guidance and wisdom. Do not depend on your own persuasiveness but seek the power of the Holy Spirit to aid you.

(5) *Talk the language of the person to whom you are witnessing.*—Seek to understand his level of conversation and talk so that he will understand you. Do not use unfamiliar terms. Use illustrations from areas of his personal interest.

(6) *Demonstrate quiet concern for the one to whom you are talking.*—Under no circumstances argue with the individual. Give no pretense that you are rushing him to make a decision. If he asks you a question you cannot answer, simply tell him that you do not know. Assure him that you will seek to find the answer. Explain that faith is often essential to understanding the Bible more fully.

Deacons can be a moving force for evangelizing the community. Each will, of course, participate in reaching the non-Christian through his Sunday School class visitation plan. But beyond this, as a deacon, he will witness with zeal and devotion.

Seldom should a deacons' meeting adjourn without deacons' being given the names of unsaved persons. A high spiritual hour for each deacons' meeting is hearing reports from the deacons regarding their labors as witnesses for Christ.

Witnessing and preaching may be new to some deacons who have majored in other activities of the church. But what more rewarding service could they perform. Deacons represent a spiritual resource that can change the world.

James Russell Lowell expressed the need to assume new direction and responsibility when he wrote the poem "The Present Crisis."

> New occasions teach new duties;
> Time makes ancient good uncouth;
> They must upward still, and onward,
> Who would keep abreast of Truth.

II. Participating in Preaching

Deacons can serve with their pastors in the preaching ministry of the church. They are not to replace the pastor in his preaching role. Rather, they are to assist in an area of Christian service too long forsaken by deacons.

Sylvester Horne said of the early Christians: "With no material weapon, no organized army, no display of force, they shook the mightiest of world empires till it trembled and tottered."

Like an exploding forest fire jumping across canyon and mountain, the good news of the Messiah's coming was preached by the Christians of the first century. Preaching knew no rank or formal ordination. The cavernous gap between clergy and layman had not yet formed.

Every kind of hurdle faced those undaunted believers. The world they encountered was hostile and intolerant. But the word "failure" was unknown to them. Even when brought before political and religious rulers they did not compromise. When commanded by word and by whip to cease preaching, "they departed from the presence of the council, rejoicing that they were counted worthy to suffer shame for his name. And daily in the temple, and in every house, they ceased not to teach and *preach* Jesus Christ" (Acts 5:41–42).

1. *Preaching Central in Proclaiming*

Preaching has always been a central method of proclaiming God's message through God's men. In the years after Christ's death and resurrection, all the followers of Christ went about preaching the gospel. Why? Because he had commanded them to do so.

At Olivet, Christ gave them their marching orders—the Great Commission. He commanded: "Go ye into all the world, and preach the gospel to every creature" (Mark 16:15). He promised authority and undergirding power to those who preach his message of salvation. "But ye shall receive power, after that the Holy Ghost is come upon you: and ye shall be witnesses unto me both in Jerusalem, and in all Judea, and in Samaria, and unto the uttermost part of the earth" (Acts 1:8).

As time passed, the churches became more formal. Patterns of Christian worship began to formalize. Church buildings became more ornate. Liturgies for formal worship were established. Levels of clerical office began to evolve. Preaching began to lose some of its spontaneity and enthusiasm. Preaching became more a function of the clergy.

A favorite story that Frank H. Leavell, Baptist student leader, used to tell concerned a Scotch scientist who examined the heather bell flower under his microscope. While peering at the delicate hue and structure of the flower, an aging Scotch shepherd stopped by. When the scientist showed him the heather bell through the microscope, the shepherd gasped, "Oh to think that all these years I've trampled them under my feet." Preaching when seen in its true perspective takes on a new scope for the deacon. Many churches today are giving deacons an opportunity to get a closer look at preaching through regular opportunities to proclaim God's Word.

2. *Need for Reexamination of Deacon's Role*

We must not forget that God works in the heart of some men, calling them to preach the gospel as ordained ministers. These men, like Christ, feel that God has claimed them for this ministry. They know the meaning of the passage: "The Spirit of the Lord is upon me, because he hath anointed me to preach the gospel to the poor; he hath sent me to heal the brokenhearted, to preach deliverance to the captives, and recovering of sight to the blind, to set at liberty them that are bruised, to preach the acceptable year of the Lord" (Luke 4:18–19).

The deacon, ordained to service, too can speak out for God. Pastors and deacons can examine the place of the deacon in preaching. Like Amos, the shepherd, the deacon can say: "The Lord God hath spoken, who can but prophesy?"

The Bible provides many descriptions of preaching, most of which are far from today's concept of a formal, prepared sermon to be delivered. Several Greek words are used in the New Testament in reference to the types of preaching done by Christians. There is the method of simply *telling*. Repeatedly, references are made in the

Scriptures to quiet conversation about a personal encounter with Christ. At other times preaching is characterized as "bearing witness," "testifying," "teaching," or "evangelizing."

There is a place for deacons to serve Christ in any of the patterns of preaching.

3. *Ways Deacons Participate in Preaching*

As churches give more emphasis to deacons' participation in the preaching ministry, creative approaches are being used to involve the deacon more fully.

A deacon once remarked to me about his experience of preaching for several Sundays in a new mission. "I don't know whether I got across to them what was in my heart. But I'll never be the same again since feeling the responsibility for the spiritual welfare of those people."

Deacons are being used more widely for leading the Sunday and Wednesday evening services. When the pastor is away, a deacon can serve as leader and preacher. He knows the needs of the people, and they know his compassionate concern for them. Preaching is a heart-to-heart encounter—not simply the polished delivery of a prepared sermon.

Some churches are using deacons to preach in missions or chapels that are sponsored by the church. Deacons can serve until a minister is secured.

Many pastors work closely with the deacons in church revival preparation. Dates, revival leaders, special emphases are discussed. Then the pastor and the chairman of deacons take these tentative plans to the church council meeting for evaluation. In the church council, other council members suggest the distinctive contribution the organization they represent can make to the church revival preparation.

Prerevival visitation by deacons has been another widely accepted project. During visits, the deacons encourage families to attend the revival services. Deacons also pray specifically for individuals to make a decision for Christ. The *Evangelism Plan Book* and *Pastor's Guide for a One-Week Revival* by John F. Havlik and Robert G. Witty are helpful resource books for deacons as they participate in revival preparation.

Some pastors also counsel with the deacons regarding persons to fill the pulpit in the pastor's absence. In churches where deacons serve in this capacity, a church pulpit supply committee is not needed.

4

Lead the Church to Perform Its Tasks

DEACONS have a responsibility for serving their church in a distinctive manner.

This chapter interprets the deacon's work that grows out of two church pastoral ministries tasks: (1) lead the church to engage in a fellowship of worship, witness, education, ministry, and application, and (2) lead the church in performing its tasks.

I. BUILDING AND MAINTAINING CHRISTIAN FELLOWSHIP

Building and maintaining Christian fellowship is at the heart of the deacon's task today. The enrichment of fellowship should rank as one of the deacon's primary concerns. This responsibility places him in close harmony with the original purpose of the "seven" men who were appointed by the church in Jerusalem. These early prototypes of today's deacon were charged with the task of healing the potential break in Christian fellowship. Pastor and deacons today confer regularly regarding matters related to church fellowship.

Sidney W. Powell in *Where Are the People?* (New York: Abingdon-Cokesbury Press, 1942) tells of a man who went into a church and was met by a deacon. "It was his handshake that got me," he said. "I was won by a handshake. It was something about the way he took my hand in his, rather than the word he spoke, that made something happen in my soul and led me to Christ."

Fellowship is far more than a friendly handshake. But a warm handclasp that radiates Christian love comes only from togetherness in Christ.

Paul had experienced the hand of fellowship, and he reminded his followers to build up and maintain this Christian spirit. "And when James, Cephas, and John, who seemed to be pillars, perceived the grace that was given unto me, they gave to me and Barnabas the right hands of fellowship; that we should go unto the heathen, and they unto the circumcision" (Gal. 2:9).

On another occasion Paul wrote of the fellowship of Christians: "No more strangers and foreigners, but fellow-citizens with the saints, and of the household of God" (Eph. 2:19). Such a pervading spirit of Christ within a church binds people together with an unseen togetherness so that they are one in mind, spirit, and body. The Greek word *koinonia* is used repeatedly throughout the New Testament to describe the oneness that Christians should experience.

Persons are no longer strangers and foreigners when they worship together. Instead they are bound together as citizens of a new nation. They take on the characteristics of family members. They have a new love and appreciation for others that overlooks superficial blemishes.

Deacons can serve their church by interpreting the necessity for maintaining the spirit of Christ in fellowship. This can be done in a variety of ways that range from a churchwide emphasis to special deacon-led activities that focus on fellowship.

Each word that is uttered by a deacon should be tempered with Christian love. His conversation will be monitored by those who look to the deacon for spiritual direction. Words of harsh criticism or gossip should be foreign to him. He should speak highly of his church, pastor, Christian friends, and neighbors.

Deacons should understand the relationship of discipline to Christian fellowship.

Loving discipline is essential to the maintenance of fellowship. Christ called for complete discipline on the part of his followers. Discipleship and discipline are close kin. The requirements of Christian discipline demand obedience to Christ.

Christian fellowship cannot long exist unless each person is willing to give himself in redemptive love so that others may grow more like Christ. Discipline is essential to the establishment and maintenance of Christian fellowship.

Earl Waldrup said in *New Church Member Orientation Manual* (Nashville: Convention Press, 1965): "Discipline is both formative and reformative. Formative discipline is the process by which a church inspires, guides, educates, and strengthens its members. Reformative discipline is the corrective and redemptive process by which a church seeks to restore wayward members to the fellowship, or exclude them when restoration fails. Its purpose is to protect the integrity and vitality of the church's witness and possibly by such action regain the wayward brother."

The work of the deacon provides an opportunity for him to demonstrate love and concern for the welfare of persons in need. Until a church provides formative discipline in the spirit of love, it cannot provide reformative discipline in a spirit of love.

A church needs a setting in which potential breaks in

Christian fellowship can be examined in a spirit of love.

Hershel H. Hobbs, former president of the Southern Baptist Convention, says: "Primarily church discipline is to be positive rather than negative. It is to be preventive and curative rather than destructive. In the New Testament church discipline was related to purity of doctrine, unity of fellowship, and holiness of its members."

Daniel B. Weaver, Baptist pastor, once shared some insights regarding the deacon's role in assisting to resolve problems of discipline. He suggested these ways:

"(1) Deacons should not give members in their care the feeling that the deacon is their moral supervisor. This would hinder the real purpose of spiritual encouragement and counsel intended.

"(2) Acute irregularities should be approached by the deacons as a body in regular assembly for the purpose of prayer and consultation among the deacons.

"(3) When it is deemed wise, the deacons may appoint a special committee to visit and counsel with the member involved. Correction of the irregularity and restoration to right relationship with the church should be the aim of all such visits.

"(4) After New Testament procedures are prayerfully followed and when they fail to restore delinquent members, and when it is deemed wise, the deacons may refer the matter to the church for further action.

"(5) Deacons should be slow to listen to gossip or any critical attitudes . . . always encouraging the party involved to pattern his or her thinking in line with the words of Christ: 'He that is without sin among you, let him first cast a stone at her.'"

Deacons can be helpful by stressing the need for their church to develop certain guidelines and tools that assist in maintaining fellowship.

A church constitution and bylaws, for example, are helpful tools for preventing a break in fellowship. Deacons alone should not develop a church constitution and bylaws, but they can call to the attention of the church the need for these tools. The constitution and bylaws should be approved by the congregation. Materials to help in writing a church constitution and bylaws may be obtained from the Church Administration Department, Baptist Sunday School Board, 127 Ninth Avenue, North, Nashville, Tennessee 37203.

What are the values of a constitution and bylaws? How does such a document assist in maintaining fellowship?

Allen W. Graves, dean, School of Religious Education, Southern Baptist Theological Seminary, listed some of the values in a *Church Administration* article (October, 1961).

> One of its main values is the opportunity it gives the church to look at itself; to redefine its purposes, objectives, and procedures; and to evaluate the effectiveness of its organizational structure. . . .
>
> If the church has worked out carefully a constitution and bylaws that is in general accord with other such documents, it can be guided wisely by it when differences of opinion arise among the members of the church. . . . By anticipating the various types of difficulties that may arise and providing for their orderly disposition in the constitution and bylaws, conflicts involving personalities can be prevented. Where differences of opinion arise over procedure and no constitution exists, there may result a serious breach of Christian fellowship.

A stated church covenant, policies and procedures,

and job descriptions for all church staff, and suggested duties for church-elected officers and committees are also helpful tools for preventing misunderstandings which lead to broken fellowship. Here again, the deacons alone should not develop these, but they should call attention to the need for them. For example, the church personnel committee should prepare the staff job descriptions, and the church nominating committee should prepare the suggested duties for the church officers and committees.

II. Improving Corporate Worship

The improvement of congregational worship is an area of work that provides unlimited opportunity for deacons. Deacons have a responsibility to lead others to follow the scriptural admonition: "It is written, Thou shalt worship the Lord thy God, and him only shalt thou serve" (Luke 4:8).

Before deacons can lead others to worship more meaningfully, each of them must experience a spiritual renewal that reflects itself in an abiding love for his church. Pastor Charles J. Granade tells of a deacon he knows.

"One Saturday afternoon I was in the study of the church. When I heard someone walking through the building, I went out to see who it was. It was one of the deacons. When I asked him if there was anything I could do for him, he replied: 'I often come to the church and walk about or sit and meditate. I love every brick in this building. I love the mortar between the joints. I love the plaster on the walls.' He could say like the psalmist: 'How amiable are thy tabernacles, O Lord of hosts! My soul longeth, yea, even fainteth for the courts of the

Lord: my heart and my flesh crieth out for the living God' (Psalm 84:1–2). From this deacon I have learned to have a greater love for the house of God."

1. *What Is Worship?*

Persons who comprehend its meaning and values understand that worship is the highest and noblest privilege that the redeemed can attain.

Franklin M. Segler says in *A Theology of Church and Ministry* (Nashville: Broadman Press, 1960): "True worship furnishes the motivation and the power for living, witnessing, and serving. When worship dies, all the other functions of the church die, for the life of the Spirit is no longer in the church."

Gaines S. Dobbins in *The Church at Worship* (Nashville: Broadman Press, 1962) adds another dimension when he says: "Worship in and of itself possesses no magic powers. Vital worship relates man to God, and the source of power, that through man his power may be made manifest. The restoration of worship to its original purity and power is important far beyond maintaining the propensity of the churches—it is at the heart of the solution of the problems of human survival."

Worship is one of the basic functions of a church. What can deacons do to enrich corporate worship in their church? How can they enhance true worship on the part of the congregation?

2. *How Deacons May Assist*

One way is by participating personally in worship opportunities that are provided. The deacon's presence will testify to others that he, like the psalmist, says in his heart: "I will bless the Lord at all times: his praise shall continually be in my mouth. . . . O magnify the Lord with me, and let us exalt his name together" (Psalm 34:1, 3).

Deacons can also serve their church through wise evaluation of worship services. Working closely with the pastor, deacons can search for ways to improve the atmosphere for worship.

Many ingredients are involved in developing an atmosphere that is conducive for corporate worship. Architecture has a major influence on persons. Cleanliness and care of the building and equipment is important. Scripture reading and prayers add depth and meaning to the worship service. The conduct of ushers in greeting persons, and the receiving of tithes and offerings can add to the atmosphere of worship. The ordinances of baptism and the Lord's Supper can be meaningful worship experiences when properly conducted.

Training sessions on the values and elements of worship can be exceedingly helpful for the deacons. Discussion regarding their evaluation of the worship services can follow the training sessions. The deacons would profit from these discussions.

Since deacons share in the pastoral ministries of a church, they will sometimes have the opportunity to lead in the worship services. Their role may vary. They may lead in officiating, praying, reading the Scriptures, preaching, ushering, or assisting in the ordinances. Whatever the occasion, the deacon should remember the lofty responsibility that he bears. Like Paul, he will need to say: "Let the word of Christ dwell in you richly in all wisdom; teaching and admonishing one another in psalms and hymns and spiritual songs, singing with grace in your hearts to the Lord. And whatsoever ye do in word or deed, do all in the name of the Lord Jesus, giving thanks to God and the Father by him." (Col. 3:16–17).

III. Administering the Church Ordinances

Deacons assist in administering the Lord's Supper and baptism ordinances. The deacon's participation in these ordinances demonstrates graphically the spiritual ministry that the church has ordained him to perform.

1. *Understanding the Meaning of the Lord's Supper*

An understanding of the meaning of each ordinance is essential to the fullest understanding of the deacon's role in them. One of the clearest interpretations of the Lord's Supper is given by M. E. Dodd in his book *Christ's Memorial* (Nashville: The Sunday School Board of the Southern Baptist Convention, 1934). To him the ordinance was "a proclamation of a past act, the pronouncement of a present experience, the prophecy of a future event. Those who sit at the Lord's table are to turn their eyes of faith back to the cross, are to lift up their open eyes of hope to Christ's coming again, and are to open their hearts to fellowship with his Spirit. The Lord's Supper deals with believers in three tenses—past, present, and future. As to the past, it is a commemoration; as to the present, it is a meditation; as to the future, it is an anticipation. . . . Each communicant at the Lord's table who partakes of the broken bread and who drinks from the cup becomes a mute messenger to the truth of the everlasting gospel 'that Christ died for our sins according to the Scriptures.' The Lord's Supper speaks a universal language, and those who observe it proclaim a universal message."

2. *Serving the Lord's Supper*

Deacons share the responsibility for the Lord's Supper to be a time of spiritual renewal for those Christians who participate. The supper is a memorial of love and fellowship. Its true meaning should not be lost in ritualism and ceremony or by haphazard administration. Simple beauty and dignity should characterize the observance of the ordinance.

Planning is essential if the ordinance is to achieve its true purpose. An experienced pastor can provide wise counsel as preparation is made for providing training for the deacons who will make ready and serve the Lord's Supper.

Adequate and proper organization should be established so that the elements are prepared early and are ready for use when needed. The Lord's Supper service materials need to be appropriate, clean, and in good repair. Training in proper serving procedures is imperative if each deacon is to know his exact assignment. Knowledge of his work and confidence in being prepared adds worshipful dignity to the service.

3. *Understanding the Meaning of Baptism*

Deacons also share the responsibility for making the ordinance of baptism a meaningful experience for the candidate and for the worshiper. An understanding of the full meaning of this ordinance will be helpful to the deacon.

Baptism was ordained by Christ as an ordinance symbolizing his death and resurrection. He assumed the burden of human guilt. His baptism visualized his death because of this guilt and his raising up from the water symbolized his resurrection. Christ's death, burial, and resurrection from the dead are symbolized by the ordinance of baptism. Both tragedy and triumph are proclaimed in this memorial. Baptism cannot save a sinner. Instead, it pictures the change that has already taken place in the soul of a person who has accepted Christ as his Lord and Saviour. The Scriptures picture this experience: "Therefore we are buried with him by baptism into death: that like as Christ was raised up from the dead by the glory of the Father, even so we also should walk in newness of life" (Rom. 6:4).

4. *Preparing for the Baptism Service*

Deacons share the responsibility for making preparation and follow-through for the baptism service. Training should be given to those deacons who are appointed to serve in this responsibility during the church year. Baptism should be a time of rich spiritual experience for the participant. When deacons make adequate preparation and perform their responsibilities properly, they serve their Lord and their church.

IV. Setting a Personal Example in Everyday Living

Paul's advice to Timothy can serve as counsel for deacons, for they too are to set a personal example in their daily living. Paul said: "Be thou an example of the believers, in word, in conversation, in charity, in spirit, in faith, in purity" (1 Tim. 4:12).

A portion of chapter 1 of this book is devoted to the

qualifications that deacons should possess. Regardless of a person's maturity, he can continue to grow spiritually by seeking to find and do the will of God.

A haughty and hostile world watches the deacon. Young Christians look to him for spiritual guidance. He needs always to be on guard, for he is an example to someone.

His daily conversation should be above reproach. Gossip must be unknown to him. Slander and unbecoming language are not a part of his nature.

His personal example indicates he is a man of Christian charity and love. He thinks of others rather than of himself. His compassion for persons grows out of his love of God and his fellowman. He does not focus attention on himself, but his deeds speak of his charitable nature.

Humility and kindness characterize him. He accepts persons for what they are and for what they can become. His spirit is such that one feels the presence of God when he is near. People enjoy being around him. He does not dwell on negatives. He enjoys the light moments of Christian fellowship.

His faith reaches deep. People know that he is a man whose word is his bond. He is a man of spiritual purpose. He feels that he was born for such an hour as this.

A deacon has a responsibility to be an example through his church attendance. He should be a man who loves his church and seeks to support the total program. He returns to the Lord a portion of his possessions. He enjoys fellowship with other Christians. He is stimulated by opportunities to learn. He goes to church to prepare his soul so that he can go out to serve the Lord.

V. Interpreting the Work of the Church to Church Members and the Community

Much of the deacon's responsibility for interpreting the work of the church to church members and the community is performed through the Deacon-led Spiritual Care Program.

In order to interpret properly the work of the church to others, the deacon must first be well informed about the life and work of his church. To be informed he must have personal knowledge gained through participation.

As a deacon visits in the homes of church members and nonmembers, he will often be asked about the church's work. When questions are asked, he should answer with confidence and accuracy. Does the church have a kindergarten? If so, who is eligible to enrol? What literature is used in Sunday School? What provisions are made for young children? What are the church's objectives and goals? Is the church following a long-range plan? What is the Wednesday evening schedule? These are some of the questions the deacon should be able to answer as he interprets the work of his church.

He will also be asked what Baptists believe. Questions regarding the denomination will come to him. Inquiries will be made regarding the mission program of the church. Others will be interested in the stewardship program.

Deacons also need to know about the church's physical facilities. When persons ask about the nurseries, he should know where they are located and who are the leaders. Questions regarding parking facilities should not baffle him. He needs to be a ready resource person on significant questions regarding the church's future plan for facilities.

Knowledge about persons in the church membership is also important. It is impossible, of course, for the deacon to know each person by name. But he needs to know the names of church leaders and as many of the members as possible. The Deacon-led Spiritual Care Program provides him many opportunities to know individuals and families intimately.

Training sessions can be helpful to aid the deacon in better understanding his church. The church as a spiritual organism and as an organization can be interpreted. The purpose of church program organizations and church officers and committees can be clarified. The church budget, policies and procedures, church covenant, church constitution and bylaws, committee responsibilities, staff job descriptions, and the history of the church are areas in which orientation can be given.

Deacons represent their church in all contacts they make. A well-informed deacon is an able interpreter of the work of his church to church members and the community.

5

Care for Church Members and Other Persons in the Community

Pastor and deacons share in the ministry of providing care for church members and other persons in the community. Care is primarily a pastoral service. The scope of the work is so great that a pastor cannot possibly do all that is required. The "seven" of the Jerusalem church were closely related to a service of this nature. Other church leaders relate to the care of persons, but the pastor, staff, and deacons have a central role in this service.

Providing care of families is an essential element in the nature of the church. Jesus gave primary attention to meeting the needs of persons during his ministry on earth. His church continues his example.

Paul often spoke to the churches about their concern for persons. He wrote: "Bear ye one another's burdens" (Gal. 6:2). On another occasion he said: "But we were gentle among you, like a nurse taking care of her children" (1 Thess. 2:7, RSV).

Deacons are in a natural position to serve in distinctive areas of care of families. Some of these areas of service are: (1) encourage family worship in homes; (2) shepherd new families into the fellowship of the church; (3) witness to families; (4) meet special family needs, such as broken homes, delinquency, aging, alcoholism, crisis counseling; (5) discover families in need;

(6) alert the church council to general family needs; (7) maintain a relationship between community agencies and the church; (8) develop a sense of family responsibility in the church.

Byron A. Clendinning, family ministry section supervisor, Baptist Sunday School Board, states the definition and scope of care of families: "Care of families encompasses the full range of all that a church does in seeking to meet the needs in family relationships. This is a ministry directed toward families. Each member of a family is seen as a total person and it deals with relationships as a whole. All matters that disrupt wholesome family relationships serve as an opportunity for ministry by deacons."

Deacons seek to fulfil their obligations of caring for persons by (1) ministering in times of crisis, (2) providing pastoral counsel and referral, (3) providing vocational guidance, and (4) performing acts of benevolence.

I. Ministering in Times of Crises

In keeping with his job of performing pastoral ministries, the deacon can make a contribution of high priority by caring for the sick, bereaved, estranged, lonely, and troubled of the church family and the community.

Most pastors spend many hours each week visiting persons of the church and community who are experiencing problems. Visits by deacons do not replace the pastor's visit, but they do enable the pastor to spend more time with individuals who have the greatest need. Serving as a Christian visitor is not new for deacons, for they have performed this type of work in the past.

Albert E. Simms, Baptist pastor, told of a deacon who was well past the three-score-and-ten mark in years. "Another three-year term of service as an active deacon was about to expire, and it was proposed that he be named a deacon emeritus. His immediate though gracious reaction was given insistently. 'No, thank you, sir. I don't want to be made an emeritus deacon. I'm afraid if this happens, I won't be given a visitation list, and I want to work as long as I'm able.' This he did, serving as an active deacon, until he died at seventy-eight."

A similar incident is told by Earl Stallings, Baptist pastor, regarding a Federal judge who visited regularly for his church. "It was typical of him to call me often and ask that we go together. Probably half the people who joined our church had been visited personally by this deacon. One time we went into a low-rent housing area to visit three young boys. We found two, but another boy, a Chinese, was not at home. The judge insisted that we find him—and we finally did at the Boys' Club. He, too, was won and I baptized all three. This is a deacon par-excellence."

Some churches use a deacon-of-the-week visitation plan for meeting special needs of church members.

W. Henry Crouch, Baptist pastor, made this statement about the deacon-of-the-week plan that is used in the church where he is pastor. "The deacon-of-the-week plan aids the membership in getting better acquainted with the deacons, and the deacon, in turn, gets new insight into the needs of the people. Through this plan, the church as a whole becomes better acquainted with each deacon and his family, and is made conscious of the deacon's willingness to minister. This increases the deacon's effectiveness as a church leader.

"He receives notices of weddings, funerals, needy shut-ins, and the sick at various hospitals. His personal appearance and visits provide an additional ministry that is needed, helpful, and impressive. He thereby learns how to accept responsibility and is made to feel the weight of the personal ministry of the church.

"There are many times during the course of a year when a pastor in his own personal ministry is grateful for the presence of a dedicated deacon. Usually, emergency calls for the pastor come late at night and are lonely experiences. Our deacon-of-the-week plan places at the pastor's disposal a different deacon each week to stand beside him and share in his ministry. These experiences help the deacon to understand some of the extreme emotional tensions on the pastor and open his eyes to the tremendous possibilities of personal service through the church.

"One night, well past midnight, my telephone rang. It was a man who confessed his sins and cried for help. He had just arrived in our city. He was broke, hungry, and lost, and pleaded for interest, food, and assurance that God could forgive. I had mingled feelings as I sleepily promised to come and help.

"I then called the deacon of the week, and in a matter of minutes we were on our way together to offer assistance and to show Christian concern. This experience strengthened the deacon's Christian compassion and gave him a practical outlet for service."

Times of crises provide deacons an opportunity for Christian service that is beyond measure.

David K. Morris, Baptist journalist, relates an incident that typifies how a deacon can share his Christian witness in a time of crisis. "It was during one of those rare occasions when the pastor was out of town and could not be reached. This deacon was notified of the death of one of the church members, a faithful usher for many years. Upon learning that the pastor was away, the deacon called the family and offered his assistance. He learned that no arrangements had been made, and the widow seemed in need of help.

"The deacon went to the home of the deceased, where he spent most of the day. He comforted the family, took down vital information to send to the newspaper, checked with the funeral home concerning details, made several long-distance calls to contact pallbearers, located the pastor and checked details and assured him that all was in order, and contacted the brother of the deceased in a distant state.

"Throughout the day, the deacon greeted callers and answered the telephone. In many instances, the family called on the deacon to help make decisions during the day. He carefully and confidently assisted them in these decisions.

"By the next day, other family and friends had arrived to comfort and help the bereaved family. The deacon faded out of the picture as his services were no longer needed at that time. He was called on to be one of the pallbearers, and he served gladly.

"The pastor arrived to conduct the funeral and later expressed his appreciation to the deacon for his helpfulness. He explained to the deacon that it was this kind of service for which the deacon was suited. And the deacon agreed that the experience had drawn him closer to the family, the church, and the Lord as he participated in serving the needs of persons."

Pastoral visits are an essential service for deacons, advocates Edward E. Thornton, seminary professor. Relating his experience, he said: "A large church in Birmingham, Alabama, took the idea of the shepherding ministry of deacons seriously enough to launch a shepherding program. . . . Statistics do not tell the exciting story of discovering a widow who had been out of contact with her church for seventeen years, but who in response to the friendship of her deacon-shepherd reentered the life of the church. She said later, 'It was as if I had come back to the land of the living.'

"Statistics do not tell of the retired couple who were found without heating fuel in midwinter. The fact that they owned their home disqualified them from welfare assistance. Medical expenses had created a financial burden. The church could help because a deacon-shepherd discovered their need.

"Perhaps the most important result was in the spiritual growth of deacons themselves. Deacons, who thought themselves incapable of making a 'pastoral call,' found it easy to call in the interest of revising the church roll, interpreting the church program for the coming year, or inviting members to cottage prayer meetings and revival services. In the process, they became the church's radarscopes, locating acute needs for pastoral ministries."

Pastoral visitation can renew the spiritual fires within the deacon. As he sees the needs of persons, he realizes anew why they respond like the psalmist who lamented:

"I am forgotten as a dead man out of mind: I am like a broken vessel" (Psalm 31:12). These personal encounters can refresh the soul of the deacon and send him out with renewed spiritual strength. "Inasmuch as ye have done it unto one of the least of these my brethren, ye have done it unto me" (Matt. 25:40).

II. Providing Pastoral Counsel and Referral

Few responsibilities of the deacon require more skill and training than providing counseling assistance. Counseling is an area with a tremendous range of intensity, from the friendly word or the sympathetic ear to those cases needing psychiatric help. The deacon should learn how to recognize cases beyond his competence and have some understanding of how to get an individual to the kind of help needed. Sometimes this need can be met only by the pastor or a highly trained professional.

The extreme cases, however, should not frighten men from the needs they can meet in the areas of prevention, of handling small problems before they become larger difficulties, of providing a sympathetic ear for those who need to organize their thinking in a permissive environment.

John Charles Wynn in *Pastoral Ministry to Families* (Philadelphia: Westminster Press, 1957) warns: "Counseling, contrary to the simple popular notion, is not to be compared to a fortune-telling machine in the penny arcade where one points to the area of his question, inserts his coin, and then watches the answer light up. In counseling, we never reach the end of the assembly line and we never have perfectly fitting interchangeable parts."

1. *Requirements of a Counselor*

Developing a counselor's concern for persons and the skills for effective work can require a lifetime of training and service. But few responsibilities can be so meaningful to the deacon as laboring with his pastor in meeting the crisis needs of persons in Christ's name.

To become effective as counselors, deacons must develop a concern for persons. Like Jesus, they must reflect compassion for those in need. "When he [Jesus] saw the crowds, he had compassion for them, because they were harassed and helpless, like sheep without a shepherd" (Matt. 9:36, RSV).

Wayne E. Oates describes in *The Christian Pastor* the crises of life and the need for an understanding and skilled person to help.

> The crises of everyday living—birth, redemption, work, marriage, illness, bereavement, and death—are the shared experiences of all people in one way or another. They are the common ventures of life in which "the whole creation has been groaning in travail together until now" (Rom. 8:22). The straitening anxieties of these times of crisis call for a reorganization of the total personality of an individual and his family, and the result may easily be disorganization. These crises either strengthen or weaken an individual personality; they are either-or situations which call for ethical choice, increase in emotional maturity, and additional spiritual resources. Therefore, the careful and considerate attention of a skilled minister under the tutelage of the Holy Spirit in these crises often makes the difference between a spiritually mature and mentally healthy person and a spiritually retarded and mentally sick person.[1]

---

[1] From *The Christian Pastor*, by Wayne E. Oates. The Westminster Press. Copyright 1951, by W. L. Jenkins. Used by permission.

2. *Training for Counseling*

Deacons should rely heavily on their pastor for training and actual experience in pastoral counseling. Training sessions, led by skilled counselors, can be exceedingly helpful. In addition to learning to be more effective counselors, these training sessions can be beneficial to deacons in better understanding themselves.

Counseling requires an understanding heart, skill, and an ability to communicate with others. Communication is more than telling. Equally important in communicating is the ability to listen. The presence of God is always essential if counseling is to be effective.

Deacons might well ask themselves the questions raised by Alan Keith-Lucas, university professor, at a conference for ministers. He asked these questions:

"(1) Do we really want to help? Are we really prepared to accept the discipline, to pay the price that helping [counseling] entails? And do we really want to help? Or are we more interested in being thanked, or feeling that we are wiser than others, or being in control, or satisfying our own conscience?

"(2) Do we have the courage to help? Any idea that helping does not take the whole strength of a man is an illusion. It takes an unusual amount of courage really to face another's sorrow, neither to evade it, smooth it over nor to become involved in it. It takes courage to allow people to make the wrong decision, to face anger, even to court it, to involve ourselves in a relationship that may be full of unpleasant truths, to give of oneself without thought of reward. When the woman with the hemorrhage touched Jesus' hem, Jesus it is reported, knew that 'virtue had gone out of him' and a true helper knows this feeling. It is hard, exhausting, and difficult work.

"(3) Are we humble enough to help? Can we help without demanding that people be helped in the way we want? Are we clear that no man, no man ever, knows what is really good for another? He's lucky if he knows it for himself. Nor does a helper ever know the depth of another man's temptation or the extent of his fear. Each of us only knows our own, which was surely one of the reasons Jesus told us not to judge."

If deacons answer yes to these questions, training, experience, and self-discipline will be required in order to serve well. A ministry of service awaits the man who will launch out in this area of need.

III. Providing Vocational Guidance

An unusually fine opportunity for deacon service is in the area of vocational guidance. Other organizational units in a church share this responsibility. But the close relationship of vocational guidance to pastoral ministries provides deacons with an opportunity for effective service.

Lloyd T. Householder, former director, Program of Vocational Guidance, Baptist Sunday School Board, says: "Vocational guidance finds expression in a church as an emphasis rather than a program. Thus, it is indistinguishable except as it is expressed through the church programs."

A church has many needs in vocational guidance. Some of the more evident needs in which deacons can serve are to: (1) help persons understand the meaning of Christian vocation, (2) educate all church members to appreciate the need for vocational guidance in the church, (3) help church leaders develop skills in vocational guidance, (4) help church leaders develop skills in acquiring and using vocational guidance materials, and (5) help church leaders see values in sources for referrals.

Deacons can play a significant role in assisting the church to educate individuals in the meaning of Christian vocation and to help persons seek God's purpose for their lives and to commit themselves to that purpose.

Deacons need to understand the basic actions that are required for conducting an adequate vocational guidance emphasis in a church. Deacons have a role in performing each of these actions.

A church needs to educate in Christian vocation and occupations. Persons need to be taught the meaning of the Christian life as their Christian calling or vocation. From this base, more adequate responsibility will be found in their occupational choices. Deacons can participate personally in educating themselves and their fellow church members in the philosophy and objectives of Christian vocation and in occupational decision-making.

Deacons can also participate actively in providing guidance for occupational choice and adjustment. They can be observant for indications that individuals are searching for fulfilment through the right vocation for them. Knowledge of personality development and unique problems that individuals face at certain stages in life is exceedingly helpful to deacons.

Through intelligent and concerned counseling and guidance with individuals, a deacon can perform a needed ministry. As he visits in the homes, he has unusual opportunity to provide guidance in vocational choice with individuals and their parents. Parents need help in assisting young people in making proper decisions. Information regarding sources for referrals would assist the deacon in performing more effectively. He also needs information relative to resource materials that persons can secure. He can participate in churchwide vocational guidance retreats or conferences. Deacons can develop special vocational emphasis projects.

Another basic action for conducting vocational guidance in a church is that of nurturing decisions for church vocations. After individuals have made decisions, careful attention should be given to developing a climate in which individuals can better understand their unique abilities and developing needs. Persons facing decisions regarding vocations can respond more favorable in a wholesome climate where the leadership of the Holy Spirit can guide their lives.

As the deacons have responsibility for seeking to create a worshipful atmosphere, they are closely related to creating an atmosphere in which Christian vocational decisions can be nurtured. They need to be aware that growth of persons follows a response to a Christian vocation decision. They also should recognize that individuals may change their decisions as they obtain additional information regarding their abilities and existing needs. Informed deacons can encourage the congregation to lend their support to persons who have made decisions regarding vocations.

IV. Performing Acts of Benevolence

Performing acts of benevolence in the name of Christ is closely akin to the work of the "seven" in the early Jerusalem church. These men distributed resources to persons in need.

The benevolence work of pastoral ministries, like other areas of pastoral care, can be implemented through the Deacon-led Spiritual Care Program. If a church has such a program, a church benevolence committee is not required. Close communication should be maintained regarding the benevolence work deacons perform and the mission action programs of Woman's Missionary Union and Brotherhood, and the ministry activities of Sunday School classes. The work of these groups can be coordinated through the church council.

Deacons should be constantly alert as they visit in homes of church members and persons in the community. Evidences of physical needs may often be noted. A plan needs to be developed and followed by deacons in order to provide adequate and appropriate assistance. Needs can be reported to the program leaders of Woman's Missionary Union and Brotherhood so that these mission action programs can provide assistance. On the other hand, the needs can be of such unique nature that the deacons should provide immediate assistance.

Here are some suggestions to help deacons provide a more effective benevolence ministry.

1. *Develop Guidelines to Follow*

Decisions need to be reached regarding how much assistance will be provided. To whom will the assistance be made available? How much budget will be allocated to this ministry? Procedural steps to follow in implementing the guidelines should be determined before the ministry is begun.

When needs are discovered, they should be met quickly and by the most effective means possible. An adequate statement of guidelines will assure that appropriate help can be given by the proper person. Unless these statements are established prior to an emergency, there may be confusion and error when needs arise.

2. *Investigate All Requests*

It is wise to investigate all requests before assistance of food or clothing is made. An interview with each applicant will aid in establishing the needs that actually exist. Secure information regarding the needs, eligibility, and the amount of assistance that is required.

3. *Determine Available Community Agencies That Provide Assistance*

In cases of long-term needs, inquire into the availability of assistance from community agencies. Personal acquaintance with these agencies is essential if intelligent referrals are to be made. Interviews should be held with leaders of community agencies to determine what assistance they can provide. This information should be shared with all the deacons.

4. *Review Periodically All Assistance That Is Being Provided*

Deacons will probably not provide continuing assistance to the same persons or families. But regular evaluation of all assistance is imperative. Evaluation allows decisions to be made regarding present policies and procedures. Decisions can determine whether present assistance should be continued or terminated.

Someone should maintain a confidential file listing persons who have received assistance. Information regarding dates, amounts, and conditions requiring assistance should be kept on record.

Many churches have found it wise to establish accounts with certain business establishments in the community. They prefer to provide a certain amount of assistance rather than providing cash. Churches that give money usually have the checks written by the financial secretary or treasurer after the amount has been approved by the appropriate person. Many churches feel that it is important for a check to come directly from the church rather than from an individual.

5. *Make Monthly Reports*

Monthly reports should be made to the deacons regarding the assistance that has been given. It may be that some deacon groups prefer not to report the names of persons or families receiving assistance. In any case, the amount of money disbursed should be reported. The written records should contain all information and should be kept in confidence.

V. Providing Care Through the Deacon-led Spiritual Care Program

Special attention should be given to organizing the deacon's responsibility in providing care for persons. All members of the deacon body participate in this activity even though they may serve in another area of deacon work.

1. *Definition of Program*

Deacons use the Deacon-led Spiritual Care Program to implement the activities of witnessing, ministering during crises, counseling and referral, providing vocational guidance, and performing acts of benevolence in Christ's name.

The Deacon-led Spiritual Care Program, an organized visitation ministry, is used to reach every church family. Regular visits by concerned deacons open doors to homes, provide unparalleled opportunities for personal witnessing, strengthen church fellowship, and undergird the spiritual development of both individuals and families.

Each deacon is assigned a proportionate number of families for which he is responsible for ministering during a church year. He becomes the spiritual shepherd of these families.

At least twice a year he visits each assigned family to discuss with them the work of the church. During these visits he remains alert to crises they may be encountering. When problems are discovered that warrant the personal skill of the pastor, the deacon immediately informs him of the need.

Whenever the deacon learns that one of his group faces sickness or bereavement, he should be prompt in making a personal visit. These visits may be made at the home, hospital, funeral home, or other places where need is evident.

2. *Responsibilities of Family Care Leader*

The family care leader, who is also the chairman of the Deacon-led Spiritual Care Program, gives leadership to the program. The following six responsibilities are his:

(1) *Organize church membership into family groups.*—Each deacon is assigned a proportionate number of families. Working with the church clerk, the family care leader organizes the church membership into family groups. There will be some such as widows, college students, and single adults who alone constitute a family unit.

(2) *Organize family groups geographically.*—The family groups should be organized geographically according to the area of the church community in which the person resides. A deacon may more easily visit his group when all live in the same area. Give each deacon approximately the same number of families to visit.

(3) *Provide resource materials to deacons.*—The initial visit is more effective when the deacon has complete information about the families assigned to him. To aid him in recording relevant information a small three-ring notebook may be obtained from the Baptist Book Store. The notebook will serve as a resource for keeping pertinent information regarding the various individuals and family groups.

Deacons are usually reassigned different members each year. Ministering to different groups of families during a three-year term of service enables each deacon to know more of the members. And members have an opportunity to know a larger number of deacons.

(4) *Lead in preparation of needed materials.*—Materials that will be needed are kits for new members and letters presenting the Deacon-led Spiritual Care Program.

a. New Member's Kit.—The family care leader works in close cooperation with the church public relations committee in preparing a New Member's Kit. This kit should be given by the deacon to all persons or families who join the church. The kit may include church constitution and bylaws; church budget; church calendar; church yearbook; church policies, such as those for the Nursery and the kindergarten; talent survey record.

An attractive 9 by 12 Welcome New Member Envelope (Code 436-657) is available at Baptist Book Stores. This envelope may be used by churches in preparing the New Member's Kit.

b. Letters introducing the Deacon-led Spiritual Care Program.—First, a letter to each resident member is needed. Working closely with the church secretary or secretary of deacons, the family care leader should prepare a letter that can be signed and sent by each deacon to the person in his group. The letter should inform the person of the program; express the deacon's appreciation for the opportunity to serve him during the year; and explain his plans to visit him in the near future.

The letter should be well written and attractively duplicated. The following letter is used by Crievewood Baptist Church, Nashville, Tennessee.

Dear Church Member:

Your deacons have felt for some time that there was a need for a closer tie between the deacons and the people. We realize that the church would mean more to our people if the deacons kept closer contact with individual families. To meet this need, we have voted to divide the families of the church among the deacons. Then we will call on every family.

I take this opportunity to tell you that it will be my pleasure to serve your family as your deacon for one year. In order that we may get to know each other better, I will plan to visit in your home in the very near future.

As your deacon, I take this opportunity of service to your family gladly and quite seriously. I do hope that you will feel free to call on me to help with any problem that fits the service to which the church has elected me. If you are ill enough for the doctor, I would appreciate a call, for I am interested in you. If some tragedy comes to your family, I would like to know of it and prove my genuine Christian interest. If there is some joy that comes to you and your family, and you would like to share it, I would be happy to rejoice with you. If you have questions concerning your church, I will be happy to find the answers for you if I can.

I will look forward to my visit in your home. Just remember that we deacons want to be thought of in the same manner as your pastor in this one respect—each of us is just as near as your telephone. Feel free to call us in times of need.

Your deacon,

Second, a letter to each new member assigned to the deacon's list should be prepared. A cordial welcome should be expressed for the new member. Information regarding the member's assignment to the deacon's group should be shared. The letter also provides an opportunity to explain that the deacon will visit the home in the near future.

Crievewood Baptist Church sends this letter to members.

Dear Mr. G__________:

The church was happy to express its joy in your decision to join us during the Sunday worship service. Yet, the deacons of the church would like to express a special welcome to you. This letter is a token of our appreciation.

In this church we offer a special service. Each family is assigned to a deacon. I have been selected by your deacons to be the deacon to serve your family. I count this a happy privilege. You may expect a call from me in the next few days. I want to know you better. If there is any way that I can serve your family in my capacity as deacon, please call on me.

When we visit together, I will bring some information that the church hopes will be helpful in making it a more wholesome, friendly, and useful church to you. I believe that you will find the material that we will discuss to be both interesting and useful.

In order that you may find your place at once in our church, you will be offered some help in our weekly bulletin. It will locate for you your Sunday School class, your Training Union, and will contain a notice to you that I will have the honor of being "your deacon." In addition to this, you will find that we have all organizations of a church placed at your disposal. There is the Woman's Missionary Union and the children's auxiliaries, the Brotherhood, and the music program. We will be happy to discuss these with you when we visit together.

I am looking forward to our visit together. I know that you intend to be one of our most faithful members. Therefore, we want to offer you the finest care of any church anywhere. Many thanks for becoming one of us!

Your deacon,

(5) *Obtain name and address of new members.*—Each new member should be assigned to a deacon immediately. A visit from the deacon will be appreciated during the following week. The new member is usually responsive to a visit soon after he joins a church.

(6) *Report at each deacons' meeting.*—Prior to the regular deacons' meeting the family care leader receives reports from all deacons regarding their visitation work during the past month. As he secures these reports, he has an opportunity to counsel with the deacons regarding problems they have encountered.

The family care leader then compiles his report that will be presented to the full deacon group. He may ask deacons to share some of their experiences as they have visited in the homes of members.

6

Organize for Effective Service

DEACONS can serve their church more effectively when they are properly organized to do the work assigned to them by the church. Each existing deacon body has some type of organizational structure. The structure may be simple, with only a presiding officer and a secretary, or it may consist of an elaborate organizational framework with multiple deacon officers and leaders.

Regular study should be given to make certain that the deacon body is organized in the best manner to get its work done. The chairman of deacons should work with the pastor and deacons to develop the organization needed. The apocryphal story of the woodsman illustrates the need for getting organized to do a job. When given twelve minutes to cut down a large tree, it is said that he used the first four minutes to sharpen his ax.

I. Guidelines for Effective Organization

There are basic guidelines which, if followed, can be of help to deacons in organizing properly. Some of these guidelines are:

1. *Keep Organization Simple and Flexible*

The temptation to establish too much organization is ever present. Keep organization simple and flexible.

A large number of deacon officers and leaders is not always a sign of efficient organization. Quite the contrary! Having more organization than needed is just as bad as not having enough.

Check to see if a continuing job exists before setting up any new jobs within the deacon body. A good rule to follow is to ask if the job is one that can be performed by one deacon or a special group. After the completion of a temporary assignment, an individual or special group does not continue as a permanent part of the organizational structure.

Maintain flexibility of organization. Organize so that the structure can be enlarged or decreased according to the work to be accomplished. When a new assignment is made, for example, it is not always necessary to involve several persons. An individual leader may be able to handle the assignment alone. If the assignment reaches a point where several persons are needed regularly, the group leader can enlarge his group. Flexibility characterizes effective organization.

2. *State Duties in Writing*

If a job is significant enough to be assigned, it is sufficiently important to be put into written form. The discipline of writing out an assignment provides benefits to the total deacon body and to the person or group receiving the assignment.

Writing out a list of duties usually insures that all parts of the assignment are included. Overlapping with other existing jobs is eliminated.

A written description of duties also serves as an aid to the one receiving the assignment. It permits occasional review to see if all is being done that was assigned.

3. *Establish Proper Relationships*

A baseball player manning second base must know the first baseman's job as well as his own. Otherwise, there wouldn't be much teamwork and resultant double plays. Likewise, each deacon officer or group member should also understand the assignment of other deacons.

Deacons should have a proper understanding about reporting the results of their work. A deacon group reports on its work to the total deacon body rather than to the congregation as does a church committee. This is in keeping with the administrative principle that a group report to its parent body.

4. *Report Regularly*

Reports from deacon officers should be made with regularity to the total deacon body. Reports should be called for at each meeting. When a report is not given for two or three meetings, there is strong evidence that sufficient work was not assigned initially or that the assignment is not being done.

After a report has been presented to the deacons, a typed copy should be provided the secretary of deacons for inclusion in the minutes of the deacon group.

II. Organization and Suggested Duties of Deacon Body

The pattern of organization for the total deacon body should reflect all the work that has been assigned by the church. The following organizational charts demonstrate four patterns that churches of various sizes can use as a guide to develop an organization pattern to meet their individual needs.

The suggested pattern begins with a single organization, using only a chairman of deacons. A secretary and an associate chairman of deacons are next proposed. Individuals are then suggested to serve as leaders of aspects of deacon work in areas of proclamation, community relations, family care, and church fellowship. As the work load increases, other deacons can be assigned to assist these leaders.

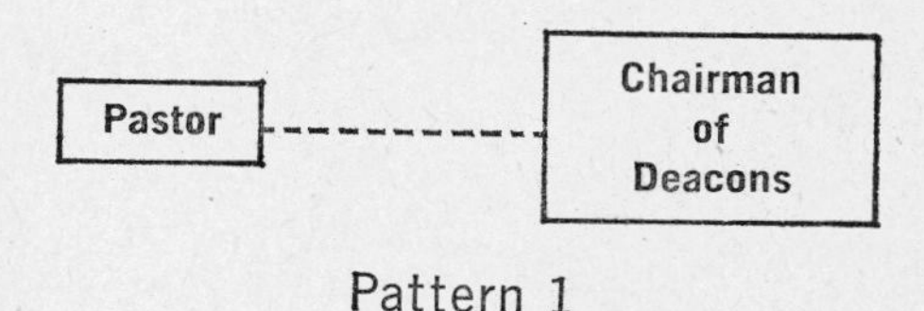

Pattern 1

The most basic plan of deacon organization begins with one officer—the chairman of deacons. When he is elected, he represents the initial organization of the deacons.

He works closely with the pastor and other deacons in planning, conducting, and evaluating the total work assigned by the church. He also serves as secretary if he is the only deacon officer. He leads out in recommending the need for additional organization as the work and number of the deacons increases.

The chairman of deacons is more than a presiding officer. He should exemplify the spiritual qualities of a stalwart Christian leader. He has a unique opportunity for close association with his pastor. Bonds of personal appreciation and fellowship should bind the two as they work together.

The chairman of deacons should be a man of patience, compassion, and mature judgment. He needs the capacity to listen with Christian concern, and the ability to maintain absolute confidence.

In planning for deacons' meetings, the chairman should confer closely with his pastor, for the two share a common task. To emphasize the concept of colaborers in a spiritual ministry some churches have begun calling the monthly meeting the pastor-deacon meeting.

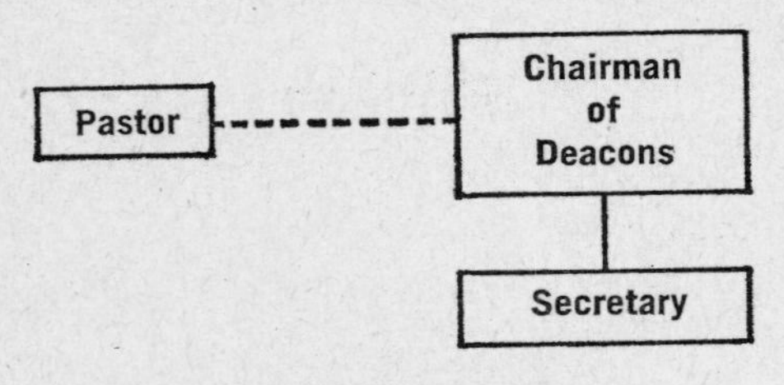

Pattern 2

SUGGESTED DUTIES OF DEACON OFFICERS

(1) Chairman of Deacons

a. Lead the deacons in planning, coordinating, conducting, and evaluating the deacons' work.
b. Plan and conduct the deacons' meeting.
c. Confer with the deacon officers as their special work is planned, coordinated, and evaluated.
d. Plan and implement training of deacons.
e. Report regularly the progress of deacon work to church.
f. Serve as a member of the church council.

(2) Secretary
   a. Keep accurate minutes and records of work.
   b. Compile deacon reports.
   c. Maintain deacon membership records and record of deacon rotation.
   d. Prepare official correspondence for deacon body.
   e. Compile the ordering of deacon literature and supplies according to church plan.

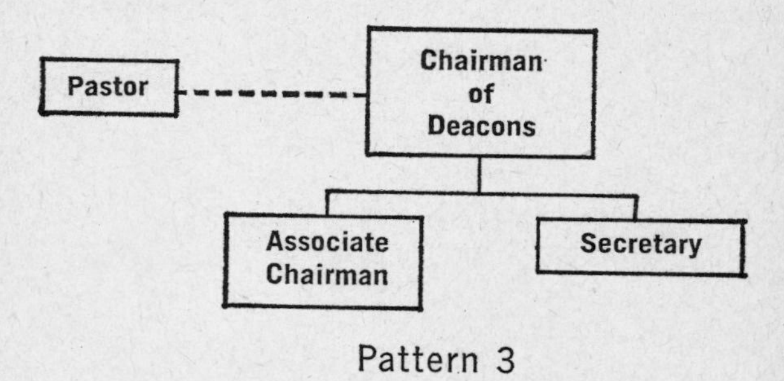

Pattern 3

SUGGESTED DUTIES OF DEACON OFFICERS

(1) Chairman of Deacons
   Duties listed on page 88.
(2) Secretary
   Duties listed above.
(3) Associate Chairman
   a. Serve as moderator for deacons' meeting in absence of chairman.
   b. Coordinate the preparation of Lord's Supper elements and properties.
   c. Coordinate the preparation and observance of baptism. (Deacons' wives can be enlisted to assist female candidates for baptism.)

d. Assist the chairman to plan and implement deacon training.
e. Assist the chairman to plan, coordinate, conduct, and evaluate the deacons' work.

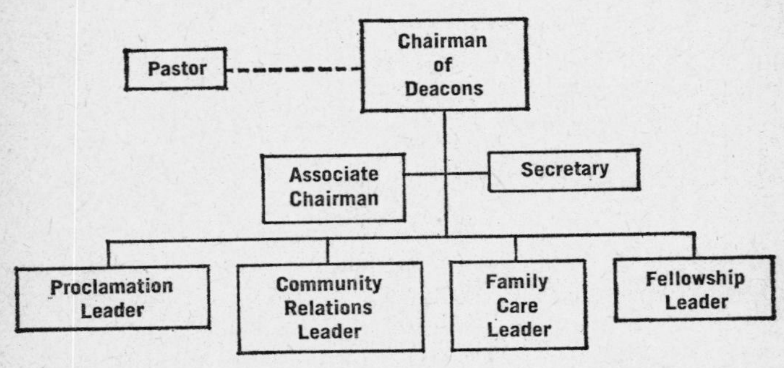

Pattern 4

SUGGESTED DUTIES OF DEACON OFFICERS

(1) Chairman of Deacons
Duties listed on page 88.
(2) Associate Chairman
Duties listed above.
(3) Secretary
Duties listed on page 89.
(4) Proclamation Leader
a. Discover opportunities for deacons to witness and preach.
b. Lead in planning and implementing witnessing and preaching activities.
c. Lead in planning and implementing deacon involvement in revival meetings.
d. Enlist deacons to participate in witnessing and preaching activities.

e. Secure resources for witnessing and preaching activities.

f. Report regularly on work to deacon body.

(5) Fellowship Leader

a. Discover opportunities for improving church fellowship.

b. Lead in planning and implementing activities for improving communication among church members.

c. Lead in planning and implementing activities to increase church concern for discipline.

d. Enlist deacons to participate in activities to improve church fellowship.

e. Secure resources for fellowship improvement activities.

f. Report regularly on work to deacon body.

(6) Family Care Leader (Chairman of Deacon-led Spiritual Care Program)

a. Discover opportunities for providing care for families.

b. Lead deacons in providing care for individuals and families in time of crises.

c. Lead deacons to give counsel to individuals and families with specific problems.

d. Lead deacons to provide vocational guidance.

e. Lead deacons to provide benevolence care for individuals and families in need.

f. Secure resources for family care activities.

g. Report regularly on work to deacon body.

(7) Community Relations Leader

a. Discover opportunities for strengthening church and community relationships.

b. Lead in planning and implementing deacon involvement in moral action in the community.
c. Lead in planning and implementing deacon involvement in civic responsibilities.
d. Lead in planning and implementing other deacon activities to improve church and community relations.
e. Enlist deacons to participate in community relations activities.
f. Secure resources for community relations activities.
g. Report regularly on work to deacon body.

7

Deacon Election, Ordination, and Rotation

A CRUCIAL PART of running any race is the ability to get off to a good start. Getting started well through proper election, ordination, and rotation is important to a church and its new deacons.

A church should use the process of deacon election that is acceptable to a majority of the church members. When a decision is made regarding a preferred method of election, it should be followed precisely.

I. Methods of Selection and Election

Churches follow a variety of plans for electing deacons. The two most widely used basic patterns are interpreted here. There are, of course, many variations of these two patterns.

1. *Suggested Pattern I—Congregation Elects by Ballot*

Some churches believe that the election of the "seven" in Acts 6:5 provides a good pattern to follow today even though the book of Acts does not refer to the "seven" as deacons. Churches following this pattern of election believe that as the multitude of disciples came together and elected the "seven" so the congregation today should choose and elect all deacons.

Variations of this plan are used, but the following pattern contains most of the basic elements.

Prior to the actual church election, every effort is made to interpret to church members the required qualifications and duties of deacons.

A list of adult male members of the congregation is prepared. The only names usually omitted from the list are persons who have requested that their names not be listed and those who are not eligible by virtue of having just completed a term of three years as deacon or who are now serving as active deacons with unexpired terms of service.

Churches mailing out a weekly bulletin often insert this list of names as a sample ballot. Members are urged to study the names and prayerfully determine their choice prior to the time for voting. Special attention is called to the spiritual qualifications a deacon should possess. Members are asked to come to church on the next Sunday prepared to vote for the required number of men that they believe are qualified for deacon service.

On the following Sunday, the printed order of service or a special ballot lists each name. As a part of the worship service, the ballots are marked after appropriate Scripture passages are read and a prayer is offered for God's guidance. Members are asked to circle a specific number of names. The deacons or ushers collect all ballots and give them to the chairman of deacons.

Following the service, the ballots are counted by a special committee of deacons. Persons counting the ballots are asked not to share the vote results with anyone. Only one list is prepared, and this is given to the chairman of deacons.

The chairman of deacons then informs the pastor of the results of the vote. These two men then contact each person elected. Starting with the person who received the largest number of votes, each is told of the confidence the church has demonstrated in him. He is not told the exact number of votes he received or how he ranked in the balloting. Deacon qualifications and duties are discussed with him. If he agrees to serve, the second man is contacted. If an individual declines to serve, other persons on the list are contacted until the required number is secured.

2. *Suggested Pattern II—Church Nominating Committee Recommends*

Many churches prefer to follow the same procedure for electing deacons that they use for electing all other church officers. First, the church nominating committee searches the total church membership for qualified men. Most nominating committees welcome the recommendation of names for consideration. To secure wider involvement, many nominating committees place deacon recommendation record forms in the church bulletin, inviting members to submit names of persons they believe are qualified to serve. The church bulletin usually lists the qualifications for deacons as well as the duties that deacons perform so that persons making recommendations may know what the church expects deacons to be and do.

If the nominating committee is to perform its responsibility well, the church should first decide and put in writing the qualifications that men should have attained if they are to be considered for deacon election. With an established standard for evaluation, the committee can more objectively make its recommendations.

After the nominating committee makes its decision regarding each person, the individual is then interviewed. Deacon qualifications and duties are discussed. If the person qualifies and agrees to serve if elected, his name is presented to the church for election.

II. Understanding Ordination

1. *Significance of Ordination*

A service of ordination, though not required for a deacon, should be a meaningful service for him, his family, and the congregation. Through ordination, a church says to those deacons it has selected: "We have confidence in your spiritual qualities and your devotion to Christ."

An understanding of the significance of the traditional laying on of hands in an ordination service adds to the meaning of the service.

Through the ages, man's hands have symbolized levels of his attainment. Time and again the Bible refers to the hands of man as a symbol of his personality. For example, a man who is acceptable to God is represented as "he that hath clean hands" (Psalm 24:4). Jesus often laid his hands on persons when he healed them miraculously by his touch.

The ceremony of laying on of hands is one of ancient beginning. In the Old Testament this practice is mentioned in connection with the Levites. The children of Israel "put their hands upon the Levites" (Num. 8:10–11). This ceremony in no way imparted any special power or authority. Rather, it stressed that these men were dedicated to God's service.

The practice of ordaining deacons probably developed from the traditional view that the "seven" in Acts 6:1–8 are the forerunners of today's deacons. The Scriptures seem to indicate that the total congregation laid hands on these men. The question is often raised today as to why other church officers such as the Sunday School superintendent are not ordained since they too hold a place of significant spiritual leadership. Some churches have an installation service for deacons rather than an ordination service. Other church-elected officers are included in the installation service for them.

Ordination in no way imbues mystical power or authority to a deacon or a minister. Gaines S. Dobbins says in an article in *Church Administration* (December, 1960): "At opposite poles from the Catholic concept is our Baptist view of ordination and the laying on of hands. We do violence to the New Testament and to our Baptist genius when we impute to the ceremony the conferring of any special qualities or rights. Anything in a Baptist church that an ordained man is authorized to do can be done by an unordained man on authority of the church."

2. *Ordination Service*

The ordination service should be a high spiritual hour in the life of a church. Many churches vary the time when the service is held in order to add variety and significance. On some occasions any ordination may be a part of a Sunday morning or evening worship service. Sometimes an entire worship service may be devoted to the ordination of deacons.

Prayerful planning is an imperative if the service is

to be conducted in a reverent and worshipful atmosphere.

The music should be selected with care. Persons participating in the service need full instructions prior to the service.

Some churches present a certificate of deacon ordination to each person who is newly ordained. Certificates are available from Baptist Book Stores.

III. Understanding Deacon Rotation

1. *The Merits of Rotation*

Research indicates that the great majority of Baptist churches today practice the election of deacons for a specific period of time. Almost all churches use a three-year pattern of rotation. After this period of service ends, each person is rotated off the active deacon group. Only after one full year is he eligible for reelection.

Churches which have practiced rotation for a number of years report these merits:

(1) Provides a broader base of leadership, enabling more qualified persons to serve their church as deacons. New and refreshing concepts of service result from new leaders.

(2) Enables qualified young adults to serve. In churches that do not rotate deacons, younger adults are not provided much opportunity for serving as deacons.

(3) Emphasizes merit rather than popularity or seniority.

(4) Discourages the concept of "board of directors" from developing through continued long-time membership.

(5) Provides an opportunity to replace those who, unfortunately, have not served well.

Robert E. Naylor says in an October, 1959 *Church Administration* article:

> Rotation of deacons is no longer an experiment in Southern Baptist life, for it is used in thousands of churches. . . .
>
> There are some seeming disadvantages, we should say in fairness, in the matter of rotation. First, it may accentuate the feeling on the part of an older man that he is "being put on the shelf." . . .
>
> In the second place, the rotation principle may remove a man from the deacon group whose leadership seems irreplaceable. I have had this experience as a pastor. What will we do without the leadership of this man on our deacon group? Remember that death can do the same thing. If there is one thing that we need to learn, it is that we are all expendable. . . .
>
> The advantages of rotating those in active service far outweigh the seeming disadvantages.

The phrase "once a deacon always a deacon" is sometimes heard. If used out of proper context, this statement can be misleading. Each church needs to properly understand and adequately interpret this matter to church members in order to prevent possible future conflict.

Every deacon should be a person of Christian character and maturity prior to his election. As a Christian, he should always continue to live by the same biblical qualifications that he maintained before his election.

If a deacon is not reelected to another term of service, he does not continue as an active deacon of his church. When he joins the fellowship of another church, he is not considered an active deacon. Only when he is elected to another term of deacon service does he again become an active deacon. When reelected, he is not reordained.

2. *Guidelines for Establishing and Maintaining Rotation*

The decision whether deacons will operate under a rotation plan of service is actually a decision for the church to make, rather than the deacons. But wisdom indicates that deacons should participate appropriately in the decision. Move prayerfully and slowly since efficiency of service is secondary to harmony of Christian fellowship.

Discuss the advantages and disadvantages of rotation. Encourage discussion from persons who hold opposing views. Invite counsel from experienced persons from other churches who have operated under a rotation system. Remember that if differing opinions are voiced, they are being expressed by Christians who honestly desire to see the work of the church move forward. Do not call for a vote too hastily. Seek to secure a recommendation from the deacons that the church establish a rotation plan rather than force the plan on the deacons.

Beginning a rotation plan for deacons need not be an unpleasant experience. W. Fred Kendall, Tennessee state convention leader, discovered in an early pastorate that it can be a spiritually enriching undertaking. He has said: "In one of my pastorates nearly all of the deacons were well past middle age, and many were getting near the end of active participation in church life and community affairs because of their age.

"The community was growing rapidly. The church was expanding at a rapid rate. New leadership was being developed in every area of church life. Many fine and very capable members had united with the church, including some very choice young men. We had begun to talk about adding some new deacons and enlarging the size of the group. This led to this discussion of getting the church to consider the rotating plan of electing deacons. Immediately many said it would never be done as long as one of the very influential deacons was living. They said he would oppose it and would cause it to be defeated.

"One day I met him as I was walking along the street near his office. He was on his way to see me. He gave me a very impressive looking document on legal paper. He asked that I read it when I got back to my study and call him and tell him what I thought of it. I was almost afraid to open it and read it since I had heard so many rumors about him. When I read the paper, I was happily surprised to find that he had worked out a suggested plan for rotation and how to initiate it. It was one of the very best plans I had seen.

"What impressed me most was his deep dedication to Christ and his very unselfish attitude toward the whole matter of serving as a deacon. He also expressed a very deep appreciation and admiration for the many young men in the church. He expressed the view that it would be a sin against them and the church if they were not added to the deacons immediately. He expressed his deep love for the men with whom he had served and stated that it would bless the younger men to have the training under them and to enjoy the fellowship for the few remaining years.

"He asked me for the privilege of presenting the suggested rotation plan to the deacons at their next meeting. They accepted the plan unanimously. He was asked to present the plan to the church. The church studied the plan and they too unanimously adopted it.

"To a wonderful deacon must go the credit. He was a man of strong convictions, but he subjected his will to that of his Master and Lord. Through this spirit of dedication, he made a contribution in an hour of decision and destiny for that church that only eternity can measure."

Determine how many deacons will be required to perform the work assigned by the church. There needs to be a direct relation between the number of deacons and the work load.

To insure greater ease in operating a three-year plan effectively, the total number of deacons should be divisable by three.

3. *Deacon Rotation Schedule*

In beginning a deacon rotation plan, the initial length of service for each deacon needs to be determined. There are a number of acceptable methods for doing this job. The following suggestions are general guidelines. Using your church's regular procedure for electing deacons, vote on the total list. Rank the names by the number of votes each received. Divide the list into three equal sections by the number of votes received. Those receiving the highest number of votes are assigned a three-year term. The second highest receive two-year appointments. The lowest one third will serve for one year. Another procedure widely used by churches for determining the length of service is simply to choose the names by lot.

4. *Record of Deacon Rotation*

Accurate records are essential for proper administration of the deacon rotation system. Responsibility for establishing and maintaining the list belongs to the secretary of deacons.

Prior to the time for annual rotation, the secretary should provide the chairman of deacons a list of deacons rotating off the deacon group. Special recognition should be made to these persons for the service they have rendered over the past three years.

The church nominating committee should be notified of the deacons who, because of rotation, will not be eligible for reelection for a period of one year. Special care should be given to see that these persons are placed in other positions of leadership.

Deacon Charles E. Noland had some sound advice for rotating deacons when he wrote in a *Church Administration* article "Deacon Rotation: Rest or Test" (January, 1961):

> The test of rotation is whether you are ready to take it seriously, or whether you are ready to simply "take it easy." Instead of looking forward to a vacation, look toward the coming period as a priceless pause. . . . Maybe you need to pause and reflect, then prepare for even greater service to your church.
>
> But pause with a plan—determine what you need to do, and do it. . . . The spiritual enrichment and administrative experience you have gained as a deacon are assets much too valuable to be wasted. Let the nominating committee know that you can be counted on to take a place of service in the future.

Suggestions for the Teacher

TEACHING HELPS

A deacon's mandate is to minister. In teaching this book, you have an opportunity to challenge each deacon to fulfil his responsibility in the pastoral ministries of his church. Challenging teaching requires advance preparation. Good teaching can be made better by using the best teaching aides to stimulate learning. Several techniques are suggested for your possible use in teaching this book.

1. *Lecturing* is standing before the class talking. The lecture is used mostly to stimulate questions and discussion.
2. In *brainstorming* the class lists as many ideas as possible which relate to a given topic. Discussion is withheld until listing is finished.
3. *Assignment-report* requires individuals to do some independent work outside the class and to report their findings to the class.
4. *Role-playing* is selecting one or more persons to portray a certain idea, activity, or situation as a starter for discussion, questions, and learning.
5. *Testing* can be used at the beginning of the course to determine how much the teacher and the class members know about the subject being discussed, and at the end of the course to note the process in learning.
6. A *case study* is a report of the facts of any situation in history, literature, or real life. The class then discusses the situation in the light of the study.
7. A *panel* and/or *special resource persons* offer their knowledge and experience in order to inform and stimulate group learning.
8. *Small learning groups* (buzz groups) are divided to discuss certain assigned subjects. Each group brings a report based on its assignment.
9. *Audiovisuals* are supplementary teaching aids. Slides, filmstrips, motion pictures, records, tape recordings, charts, grafts, mimeographed materials, pamphlets, photographs, posters, chalkboard—all these can be used to enliven group participation and stimulate learning.

Chapter 1

Begin the first session by distributing a piece of paper and a pencil to each class member. Give a "word association" test. Ask each person to write his impression on the paper as soon as the word has been spoken. For example, use "football," "car," "red," "celery," . . . "deacon." Ask each one to keep this piece of paper until the last session.

Ask some of the deacons to share their present concepts of the role of the deacon.

Ask, What do church members think the role of the deacon is? Preassign a deacon the responsibility of taking a sample poll of selected church members, using a tape recorder to gather their answers. Let him play parts of the tape. Did their concept of the role of the deacon surprise you?

View the filmstrip, *The Ministry of the Deacon Today.* After the filmstrip has been shown, ask, How does the work of the deacon differ from your concept of his role?

Chapter 2

Before this session, briefly rehearse with a few class members a sample deacon "board" meeting in which the deacons spend all their time discussing "business." When the role-play is concluded, ask, How could deacons spend their time more profitably in kingdom service?

List the pastoral ministries tasks on the chalkboard. Make a large arrow, and put two-way tape on the back side. Place the arrow beside each main point (for example, PROCLAIM) for emphasis during the discussion.

Divide the class into three small groups. Ask each group to discuss a specific relationship. Ask each group to give a brief report as to how relationships may be improved.

Chapter 3

Preassign a deacon the project of determining the condition of the prospect file and the status of the church visitation (outreach) program. Ask him to report his findings to the deacons.

List on the chalkboard as many ideas as rapidly as possible concerning the type of visitation program needed. Withhold discussion until the brainstorming is finished. Then discuss the various ideas in the light of the guidelines for witnessing listed on pages 42-43.

Ask the deacons to decide on the type and the scope of visitation in which they will engage.

CHAPTER 4

Select three deacons to serve on a panel-forum with the teacher as the leader. Ask one deacon to discuss the importance of building church fellowship. Ask another to discuss how deacons can help interpret the meaning of the Lord's Supper. Ask the other panel member to relate the meaning of baptism and the deacons' responsibility for making the ordinance worshipful.

Encourage the participants to make their remarks stimulating and provoking by bringing out real problems and presenting different points of view.

Allow time for group discussion.

Encourage members to listen purposefully and to react to the panelists' ideas.

CHAPTER 5

Have the pastor prepare a case study or share one from a book on pastoral care. Invite a resource person (doctor, lawyer, psychologist) to share his experience and knowledge in helping the group analyze the problem and seek a diagnosis, prescription, and treatment.

List on a flip chart the various types of pastoral care and discuss each type.

If the group expresses the need for additional training in this area, recommend further study of a more clinical and pastoral nature.

CHAPTER 6

Draw the expanded deacon organization chart on the chalkboard. Include principles and relationships of the deacon officers in your discussion.

Mimeograph copies of the deacon officers' duties. Distribute them to each class member. Use these sheets as references for a group discussion on the duties of each officer.

CHAPTER 7

At the first session of the course, ask for four volunteers to participate in a debate on the question of deacon rotation. Assign one team the affirmative side and the other the negative. Each team may use the material in this chapter and references in the bibliography to prepare their cases. Limit the time of each speaker. Alternate the speeches between the affirmative and the negative. Instead of the usual rebuttal, the class members may prefer asking the debaters questions regarding their position.

Ask the class members to look at the list of word associations they wrote the first night and note the word they used for "deacon." Ask whether their concept of the role of deacon has changed. This assessment of the deacon's role can be used to evaluate the course of study.

CHAPTER OUTLINES

Chapter 1 Deacons Yesterday and Today

I. Deacons in the New Testament

1. Understanding the Word "Deacon"
2. Choosing the "Seven"
3. A Service Formalized

II. A Heritage of Stalwart Service

III. Qualifications for the Deacon

1. Christian Purpose
2. Spiritual Integrity
3. Proved Spiritual Maturity
4. Christian Family Life
5. Honest in Speech
6. Temperate in Living
7. Steward of Possessions

IV. Church Guidelines for Effective Deacon Service

1. Maintain Biblical Qualifications
2. Choose Men Who Can Serve Well
3. Choose Men Who Can Work Well with Others
4. Choose Men Who Will Train for Service

Chapter 2 Evolving Concepts of Deacon Service

I. Concepts Regarding Work of Deacons

1. Deacons As Board of Directors
2. Deacons As Business Managers
3. Deacons Serving in Pastoral Ministries

II. Today's Deacons and Church Tasks

1. Definition of Church Tasks
2. Definition of Church Programs and Services
3. Definition of Pastoral Ministries

III. Interpretation of Deacons' Work

1. Relation of Deacons to Pastor and Staff
2. Relation of Deacons to Administrative Services
3. Relation of Deacons to Church Council

Chapter 3 Proclaim the Gospel to Believers and Unbelievers

I. Participating in Witnessing Activities

1. Deacons Active As Witnesses
2. Deacons Skilled As Witnesses

II. Participating in Preaching

1. Preaching Central in Proclaiming
2. Need for Reexamination of Deacon's Role
3. Ways Deacons Participate in Preaching

Chapter 4 Lead the Church to Perform Its Tasks

I. Building and Maintaining Christian Fellowship

II. Improving Corporate Worship

1. What Is Worship?
2. How Deacons May Assist

III. Administering the Church Ordinances
1. Understanding the Meaning of the Lord's Supper
2. Serving the Lord's Supper
3. Understanding the Meaning of Baptism
4. Preparing for the Baptism Service

IV. Setting a Personal Example in Everyday Living

V. Interpreting the Work of the Church to Church Members and the Community

Chapter 5 Care for Church Members and Other Persons in the Community

I. Ministering in Times of Crises

II. Providing Pastoral Counsel and Referral
1. Requirements of a Counselor
2. Training for Counseling

III. Providing Vocational Guidance

IV. Performing Acts of Benevolence
1. Develop Guidelines to Follow
2. Investigate All Requests
3. Determine Available Community Agencies That Provide Assistance
4. Review Periodically All Assistance That Is Being Provided
5. Make Monthly Reports

V. Providing Care Through the Deacon-led Spiritual Care Program
1. Definition of Program
2. Responsibilities of Family Care Leader

Chapter 6 Organize for Effective Service

I. Guidelines for Effective Organization

1. Keep Organization Simple and Flexible
2. State Duties in Writing
3. Establish Proper Relationships
4. Report Regularly

II. Organization and Suggested Duties of Deacon Body

Chapter 7 Deacon Election, Ordination, and Rotation

I. Methods of Selection and Election

1. Suggested Pattern I—Congregation Elects by Ballot
2. Suggested Pattern II—Church Nominating Committee Recommends

II. Understanding Ordination

1. Significance of Ordination
2. Ordination Service

III. Understanding Deacon Rotation

1. The Merits of Rotation
2. Guidelines for Establishing and Maintaining Rotation
3. Deacon Rotation Schedule
4. Record of Deacon Rotation

BIBLIOGRAPHY

Autrey, C. E. *Basic Evangelism.* Grand Rapids, Mich.: Zondervan Publishing House, 1959.

_____. *You Can Win Souls.* Nashville: Broadman Press, 1961.

Brister, C. W. *People Who Care.* Nashville: Broadman Press, 1967.

BROWN, HENRY CLIFTON, JR. *A Christian Layman's Guide to Public Speaking*. Waco, Tex.: Word Records, Inc., 1966.

CHAFIN, KENNETH. *Help! I'm a Layman*. Nashville: Broadman Press, 1966.

DOBBINS, GAINES S. *The Church at Worship*. Nashville: Broadman Press, 1962.

_____. *Learning to Lead*. Nashville: Broadman Press, 1968.

_____. *A Ministering Church*. Nashville: Broadman Press, 1960.

DRAKEFORD, JOHN W. *Counseling for Church Leaders*. Nashville: Broadman Press, 1961.

EDGE, FINLEY B. *A Quest for Vitality in Religion*. Nashville: Broadman Press, 1961.

GRINDSTAFF, W. E. *Our Cooperative Program*. Nashville: Convention Press, 1965.

HINSON, E. GLENN. *The Church: Design for Survival*. Nashville: Broadman Press, 1967.

HOWARD, FRED D. *Interpreting the Lord's Supper*. Nashville: Broadman Press, 1966.

THOMASON, W. O., and HOWSE, W. L. *A Church Organized and Functioning*. Nashville: Convention Press, 1966.

LAUTERBACH, WILLIAM ALBERT. *Ministering to the Sick*. St. Louis: Concordia Publishing House, 1955.

LESCH, GOMER R. *Creative Christian Communication*. Nashville: Broadman Press, 1965.

MCCLELLAN, ALBERT. *Christian Stewardship*. Nashville: Convention Press, 1966.

MCCOY, LEE H. *Understanding Baptist Polity*. Nashville: Convention Press, 1964.

NAYLOR, ROBERT E. *The Baptist Deacon*. Nashville: Broadman Press, 1955.

OATES, WAYNE E. *The Christian Pastor*. Philadelphia: Westminster Press, 1951.

PEARCE, J. WINSTON. *Planning Your Preaching*. Nashville: Broadman Press, 1967.

POWELL, SIDNEY W. *Where Are the Converts?* Nashville: Broadman Press, 1958.

SCUDDER, C. W. (ed.). *Crises in Morality*. Nashville: Broadman Press, 1964.

_____. *Danger Ahead: A Christian Approach to Some Current Problems*. Nashville: Broadman Press, 1961.

_____. *The Family in Christian Perspective.* Nashville: Broadman Press, 1962.

SEGLER, FRANKLIN M. *The Christian Layman.* Nashville: Broadman Press, 1964.

_____. *Christian Worship: Its Theology and Practice.* Nashville: Broadman Press, 1967.

STANFIELD, VERNON L. *The Christian Worshiping.* Nashville: Convention Press, 1965.

TRUEBLOOD, DAVID ELTON. *The Company of the Committed.* New York: Harper & Row Publishers, 1961.

WALDRUP, EARL W. *New Church Member Orientation Manual.* Nashville: Convention Press, 1965.

WITTY, ROBERT G. *Church Visitation: Theory and Practice.* Nashville: Broadman Press, 1967.

WYNN, JOHN CHARLES. *Pastoral Ministry to Families.* Philadelphia: Westminster Press, 1957.

YOUNG, RICHARD K. *The Pastor's Hospital Ministry.* Nashville: Broadman Press, 1954.

AUDIOVISUALS

FILMSTRIPS

The Ministry of the Deacon Today. 50 frames, color, manual, recording.

Men of Good Report. 33 frames, color, manual, recording, 7 min.

Principles of Visitation. 50 frames, color, manual, recording, 7 min.

Win Your Friends. 45 frames, color, captions, manual.

Visiting the Unsaved. 50 frames, color, manual, recording, 8½ min.

The Power of a Man's Witness. 47 frames, color, manual, recording, 7 min.

Visiting the Sick and Sorrowful. 49 frames, color, manual, recording, 6½ min.

"What Baptists Believe Series." Set of 4 filmstrips, color, manuals, 2 recordings.

MOTION PICTURES

Dedicated Men. 28 min., b & w.

Answering Objections in Witnessing, Part I. 15 min., color.

Answering Objections in Witnessing, Part II. 15 min., color.
Reclaiming the Saved. 30 min., color.
I Don't Want to Get Involved. 30 min., color.
How to Witness. 15 min., color.

BROADMAN SUPPLIES

Home Visitor Card–436–703
Handbook for the Deacon Chairman–436–698
Study Guide for the Ministry of the Deacon–436–701 (Available June, 1968)
Baptismal Invitation–436–056
Certificate of Recognition Award–436–048 (General purpose)
Deacon Lapel Pin–431–371
Deacon Tie Clasp and Cuff Link Set–431–370
Deacon Tie Clip–431–369
Deacon Tie Tac–431–368
Revival Attendance Record Envelope–431–072
Baptismal Certificate–436–033
"Homes Are for Worship Too" (leaflet)–436–685
Usher's Pin–431–215
Usher's Badge–Red Plastic–431–419
Usher's Badge–Blue Plastic–431–418
Welcome Banner Tag–431–415
The Way to the Abundant Life (pocket flip chart)–435–948
Church Outreach–Ministry Report–435–412
Enlistment Postcard, Nonresident–436–573
How to Visit (flip chart)–435–956
New Church Member Certificate–436–047
Family Worship Pledge Card–436–682
Door Knob Hanger–436–661
Deacon Report on Member–436–773
Certificate of Ordination for Deacons–436–032
Baptismal Garments
Lord's Supper Supplies
Notebook Binders: 5½ by 8½ and 8½ by 11
Home Visitation Record of Decision–436–775

For Review and Written Work

Chapter 1

1. The word "deacon" comes from the Greek word ________ ________, which means ________.
2. What problem in the Jerusalem church were the "seven" men selected to solve?
3. Name the personal qualifications for deacons set forth in the Bible.
4. What are the four basic guidelines a church should remember when considering the work of deacons?
5. Name the benefits of deacon training.

Chapter 2

6. List three evidences that deacons are operating as a "board" of deacons.
7. When did the concept of deacons as business managers emerge?
8. List three evidences that deacons are serving in the pastoral work of a church?
9. How do the pastor and the deacons labor together to meet the needs of persons in Jesus' name?
10. What are the differences in responsibilities of the church council and the deacons?

Chapter 3

11. List four guidelines to aid the deacon in witnessing.
12. List three ways deacons can serve their church in proclaiming the gospel.
13. What are some words in the New Testament that are synonymous with preaching?

Chapter 4

14. The Greek word ________ is used in the New Testament to describe the oneness Christians should experience.

15. Explain the difference in formative discipline and reformative discipline.
16. What are the values of a constitution and bylaws?
17. How can deacons assist in worship?
18. What responsibility do deacons have for making baptism meaningful for the candidate and for the worshiper?

CHAPTER 5

19. Name some ways deacons fulfil their obligations of caring for persons.
20. What are the requirements of a counselor?
21. List five suggestions to help deacons in providing a benevolence ministry.
22. Define the Deacon-led Spiritual Care Program.
23. What are the six responsibilities of the family care leader?

CHAPTER 6

24. List four guidelines to help deacons organize properly.
25. What is the most basic plan of deacon organization?
26. The four suggested leaders for deacons are ________ leader, ________ leader, ________ ________ leader, and ________ ________ leader.

CHAPTER 7

27. Name the two most widely used plans for electing deacons.
28. What is the origin of deacon ordination?
29. List five merits of deacon rotation.
30. Who decides whether deacons will operate under a rotation plan of service?